Official Certified SOLIDWORKS Professional (CSWP) Certification Guide

SOLIDWORKS 2020 - 2023

David C. Planchard

CSWP & SOLIDWORKS Accredited Educator

SDC Publications
P.O. Box 1334
Mission, KS 66222
913-262-2664
www.SDCpublications.com
Publisher: Stephen Schroff

Copyright 2022 David C. Planchard

Examination Copies
Books received as examination copies are for review purposes only and may not be made available for student use. Resale of examination copies is prohibited.

Electronic Files
Any electronic files associated with this book are licensed to the original user only. These files may not be transferred to any other party.

Trademarks
SOLIDWORKS®, eDrawings®, SOLIDWORKS Simulation®, SOLIDWORKS Flow Simulation, and SOLIDWORKS Sustainability are a registered trademark of Dassault Systèmes SOLIDWORKS Corporation in the United States and other countries; certain images of the models in this publication courtesy of Dassault Systèmes SOLIDWORKS Corporation.

Microsoft Windows®, Microsoft Office® and its family of products are registered trademarks of the Microsoft Corporation. Other software applications and parts described in this book are trademarks or registered trademarks of their respective owners.

The publisher and the author make no representations or warranties with respect to the accuracy or completeness of the contents of this work and specifically disclaim all warranties, including without limitation warranties of fitness for a particular purpose. No warranty may be created or extended by sales or promotional materials. Dimensions of parts are modified for illustration purposes. Every effort is made to provide an accurate text. The author and the manufacturers shall not be held liable for any parts, components, assemblies or drawings developed or designed with this book or any responsibility for inaccuracies that appear in the book. Web and company information was valid at the time of this printing.

The Y14 ASME Engineering Drawing and Related Documentation Publications utilized in this text are as follows: ASME Y14.1 1995, ASME Y14.2M-1992 (R1998), ASME Y14.3M-1994 (R1999), ASME Y14.41-2003, ASME Y14.5-1982, ASME Y14.5-1999, and ASME B4.2. Note: By permission of The American Society of Mechanical Engineers, Codes and Standards, New York, NY, USA. All rights reserved.

Download all needed model files from the SDC Publication website www.SDCpublications.com/downloads/978-1-63057-542-7.

SOLIDWORKS 2020
SOLIDWORKS 2021
SOLIDWORKS 2022
SOLIDWORKS 2023

ISBN-13: 978-1-63057-542-7
ISBN-10: 1-63057-542-9

Printed and bound in the United States of America.

INTRODUCTION

The **Official Certified SOLIDWORKS® Professional (CSWP) Certification Guide, 2020 - 2023** is written to assist the SOLIDWORKS user to take and pass the CSWP CORE exam.

The exam and book are organized into 3 segments. The book provides exam tips, screen shots, segment format, sample problems and questions with initial and final models for each segment.

View the provided SOLIDWORKS CSWP Sample Exam folder. The folder contains a pdf with information on the following: exam details, how to prepare for the exam, how to take the practice exam, taking the exam (only for Segment 1), sample test quesitons, test answers, and helpful sites.

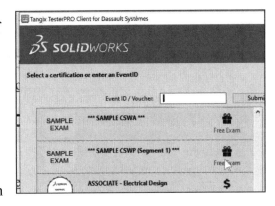

Visit https://3dexperience.virtualtester.com/#home to take the free CSWP Segment 1 sample exam using the virtualtester. An account is required.

You need to wait 30 days before you can retake the free sample exam. The sample exam ONLY addresses segment 1.

Download all needed model files (initial and final) and the SOLIDWORKS CSWP Sample Exam folder from the SDC Publications website (www.SDCpublications.com/downloads/978-1-63057-542-7

The CSWP Certification exam is offered in three separate segments. You can take any segment at any time, in any order. Once you pass a segment, you will not have to take it again.

If you fail this segment of the exam, you need to wait 14 days before you can retake that same segment. In that time, you can take another segment.

Once you pass all of the three segments, you will automatically receive your CSWP CORE Certification.

Each segment covers a different set of disciplines. All segments are timed.

Segment 1 is 70 minutes with eleven (11) questions. The format is either multiple-choice or single fill in the blank.

A total score of 75 out of 105 or better is required to pass. All answers are in the MMGS unit standard. Decimal place 2.

The first question is an instructional page. Read the instructions. Agree to the Candidate Conduct Policy. Click Yes. It's a free 5 points.

The second question is a multiple-choice format.

You should have the exact answer (within 0.5% of the stated value in the multiple-choice section) before you move on to the next question which is in a single answer format.

If you do not have the exact answer (within 0.5% of the stated value in the multiple-choice section), you will most likely fail the following question. This is crucial as there is no partial credit.

In Segment 1, create and modify parts. A question is presented to you in multiple steps.

If your school is an academic certification provider, your instructor can allocate a free exam credit for the CSWP - Segment 1, Segment 2 or Segment 3. The instructor will require your .edu email address.

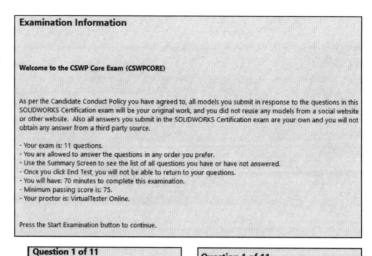
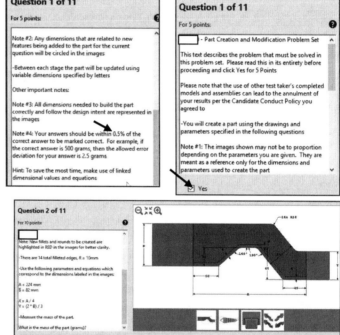
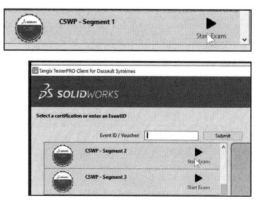

Segment 2 of the CSWP exam is 50 minutes long with twelve (12) questions divided into three categories. The segment focuses on part modifications and configurations.

The format is either multiple-choice or single fill in the blank.

The first question is an instructional page. Read the instructions. Agree to the Candidate Conduct Policy. Click Yes. It's a free 5 points.

Click the link to download the needed part files.

Save the downloaded part files to a working folder, (Extract All). Note: You should have 3 parts.

Segment 2 requires knowledge of the following:

- Download and open a zip file

- Open a part

- Apply material

- Modify specific areas of the part

- Use the Meassure and Mass Properties tool

- Apply sketch tools and sketch relations

- Recover from rebuild errors

- Understand configurations

- Create configurations from other configurations

- Modify configurations using a design table

- Recognize Engineering drawing views with annotations

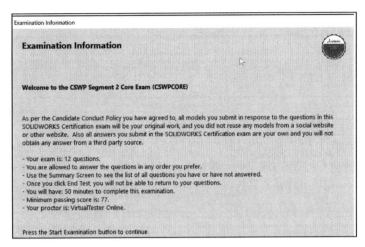

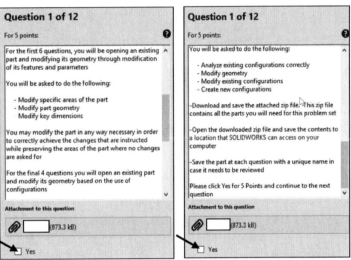

Segment 3 is 80 minutes long with fourteen (14) questions divided into three categories.

Segment 3 focuses on assemblies and modifications.

Down load the .zip folder. The .zip folder contains the needed models for this segment.

The format is either multiple-choice or single fill in the blank.

A total score of 77 out of 109 or better is required to pass.

Segment 3 requires knowledge of the following:

- Download and open a zip file

- Create an assembly

- Insert components and sub-assemblies

- Assembly and mate parts in an assembly

- Standard & Advanced (Width, Distance, Angle, etc.) mates

- Measure angles

- Mate modifications

- Suppress mates

- Move/Rotate components

- Apply Rigid and Flexible states

- Employ the Interference Detection and Collision tools

- Create and apply a new Coordinate System

- Modify and replace components

- Recover from mate errors

- Calculate mass and the center of mass

- Recognize Engineering drawing views with annotations

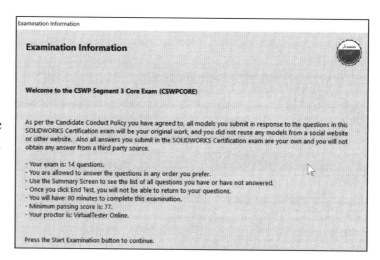

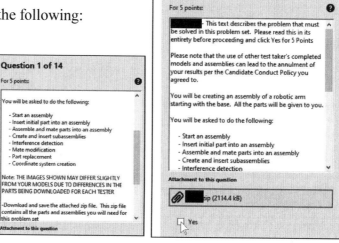

☀ During the exam, it may state: Roll Control: Free. Pitch/Yaw Control: Free. This means you can rotate freely about X, Y, and Z in the assembly.

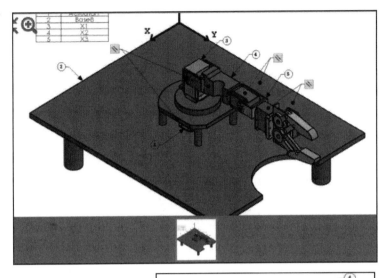

Once you pass **all three segments**, you will receive an email for your CSWP certification. Click on the SOLIDWORKS Certification Center hyperlink to login, activate and view your certificate.

☀ If you fail any segment of the exam, you need to wait 14 days before you can retake that same segment. In that time, you can take another segment.

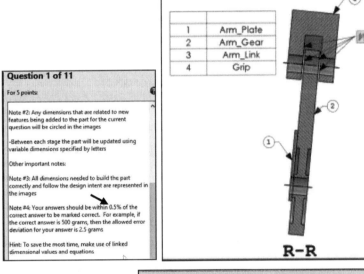

☀ If you do not have the exact answer (within 0.5% of the stated value in the multiple-choice section), you will most likely fail the following question. This is crucial as there is no partial credit.

☀ If your school is an academic certification provider, your instructor can allocate a free exam credit for the CSWP - Segment 1, Segment 2 or Segment 3. The instructor will require your .edu email address.

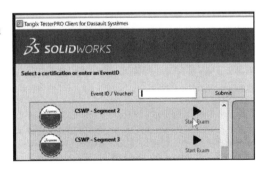

Goals

The primary goal is not only to help you pass the CSWP exam, but also to ensure that you understand and comprehend the concepts and implementation details of the process.

The second goal is to provide the most comprehensive coverage of CSWP exam related topics available, without too much coverage of topics not on the exam.

The third and ultimate goal is to get you from where you are today to the point that you can confidently pass all three segments of the CSWP exam. You must work quickly and accurately. Note: A sample CSWP Segment 1 exam is included in the book with 80 sample questions and answers to help pass the exam.

CSWP Audience

The intended audience for the book is a person who has passed the CSWA exam and has a minimum of 8 or more months of SOLIDWORKS experience and advanced knowledge of engineering practices.

About the Author

David Planchard is the founder of D&M Education LLC. Before starting D&M Education, he spent over 35 years in industry and academia holding various engineering, marketing, and teaching positions. He holds five U.S. patents. He has published and authored numerous papers on Machine Design, Product Design, Mechanics of Materials, and Solid Modeling. He is an active member of the SOLIDWORKS Users Group and the American Society of Engineering Education (ASEE). David holds a BSME, MSM with the following professional certifications: CCAI, CCNP, CSWA-SD, CSWA-S, CSWA-AM, CSWP, CSWP-DRWT and SOLIDWORKS Accredited Educator. David is a SOLIDWORKS Solution Partner, a faculty member and the SAE advisor at Worcester Polytechnic Institute in the Mechanical Engineering department.

In 2012, David's senior Major Qualifying Project team (senior capstone) won first place in the Mechanical Engineering department at WPI.

In 2014, 2015 and 2016, David's senior Major Qualifying Project teams won the Provost award in the Mechanical Engineering department for design excellence.

In 2018, David's senior Major Qualifying Project team (Co-advisor) won the Provost award in the Electrical and Computer Engineering department. Subject area: Electrical System Implementation of Formula SAE Racing Platform.

In 2020, he was awarded Emeritus status at Worcester Polytechnic Institute (WPI). His ME design class achieved world recognition, featured in *Compass* published by Dassault Systèmes, in the technical article, "Open Innovation in a Pandemic."

In 2022, David's senior Major Qualifying Project team won second place in the Provost award in the Electrical and Computer Engineering department (ECE) at WPI. His FSAE Electric team won the IEEE Excellence in Electric Vehicle Award and achieved 4th place at the Formula Hybrid + Electric competition.

David Planchard is the author of the following books:

- **SOLIDWORKS® 2021 Reference Guide** 2020, 2019, 2018, and 2016

- **Engineering Design with SOLIDWORKS® 2023**, 2022, 2021, 2020, 2019, 2018, 2017, 2016, 2015, and 2014

- **Engineering Graphics with SOLIDWORKS® 2023,** 2022, 2021, 2020, 2019, 2018, 2016, and 2015

- **SOLIDWORKS® 2023 Quick Start**, 2022, 2021, 2020, 2019, and 2018

- **SOLIDWORKS® 2023 Tutorial**, 2021, 2020, 2019, 2018, 2017, and 2016

- **Drawing and Detailing with SOLIDWORKS® 2022**, 2014, 2012, and 2010

- **Official Certified SOLIDWORKS® Professional (CSWP) Certification Guide 2020 - 2023**, 2019 - 2020, and 2015 - 2017

- **Official Guide to Certified SOLIDWORKS® Associate Exams: CSWA, CSWA-SD, CSWA-S, CSWA-AM 2020 - 2023**, 2019 - 2021, 2017 - 2019, 2015 - 2017

Acknowledgements

Writing this book was a substantial effort that would not have been possible without the help and support of my loving family and of my professional colleagues. I would like to thank Professor John M. Sullivan Jr., Professor Jack Hall, and the community of scholars at Worcester Polytechnic Institute who have enhanced my life, my knowledge and helped to shape the approach and content to this text.

The author is greatly indebted to my colleagues from Dassault Systèmes SOLIDWORKS Corporation for their help and continuous support: Mike Puckett, Avelino Rochino, Yannick Chaigneau, Terry McCabe and the SOLIDWORKS Partner team.

Thanks also to Professor Richard L. Roberts of Wentworth Institute of Technology, Professor Dennis Hance of Wright State University, Professor Jason Durfess of Eastern Washington University and Professor Aaron Schellenberg of Brigham Young University - Idaho who provided vision and invaluable suggestions.

SOLIDWORKS certification has enhanced my skills and knowledge and that of my students. Thank you to Ian Matthew Jutras (CSWE), technical contributor, and Stephanie Planchard, technical procedure consultant.

Contact the Author

We realize that keeping software application books current is imperative to our customers. We value the hundreds of professors, students, designers, and engineers that have provided us input to enhance the book. Please contact me directly with any comments, questions or suggestions on this book or any of our other SOLIDWORKS books at dplanchard@msn.com.

Note to Instructors

Please contact the publisher **www.sdcpublications.com** for classroom support materials (.ppt presentations, labs and more) and the Instructor's Guide with model solutions and tips that support the usage of this text in a classroom environment.

Trademarks, Disclaimer and Copyrighted Material

SOLIDWORKS®, eDrawings®, SOLIDWORKS Simulation®, SOLIDWORKS Flow Simulation, and SOLIDWORKS Sustainability are a registered trademark of Dassault Systèmes SOLIDWORKS Corporation in the United States and other countries; certain images of the models in this publication courtesy of Dassault Systèmes SOLIDWORKS Corporation.

The publisher and the author make no representations or warranties with respect to the accuracy or completeness of the contents of this work and specifically disclaim all warranties, including without limitation warranties of fitness for a particular purpose. No warranty may be created or extended by sales or promotional materials. Dimensions of parts are modified for illustration purposes. Every effort is made to provide an accurate text. The authors and the manufacturers shall not be held liable for any parts, components, assemblies or drawings developed or designed with this book or any responsibility for inaccuracies that appear in the book. Web and company information was valid at the time of this printing.

The Y14 ASME Engineering Drawing and Related Documentation Publications utilized in this text are as follows: ASME Y14.1 1995, ASME Y14.2M-1992 (R1998), ASME Y14.3M-1994 (R1999), ASME Y14.41-2003, ASME Y14.5-1982, ASME Y14.5-1999, and ASME B4.2. Note: By permission of The American Society of Mechanical Engineers, Codes and Standards, New York, NY, USA. All rights reserved.

Additional information references the American Welding Society, AWS 2.4:1997 Standard Symbols for Welding, Braising, and Non-Destructive Examinations, Miami, Florida, USA.

References

- SOLIDWORKS Help Topics and What's New, SOLIDWORKS Corporation.

- 80/20 Product Manual, 80/20, Inc., Columbia City, IN, 2012.

- Ticona Designing with Plastics - The Fundamentals, Summit, NJ, 2009.

- SMC Corporation of America, Product Manuals, Indiana, USA, 2012.

- Emerson-EPT Bearing Product Manuals and Gear Product Manuals, Emerson Power Transmission Corporation, Ithaca, NY, 2009.

- Emhart - A Black and Decker Company, On-line catalog, Hartford, CT, 2012.

During the initial SOLIDWORKS installation, you are requested to select either the ISO or ANSI drafting standard. ISO is typically a European drafting standard and uses First Angle Projection. The book is written using the ANSI (US) overall drafting standard and Third Angle Projection for drawings.

Download all needed model files from the SDC Publication website (www.SDCpublications.com/downloads/978-1-63057-542-7). All model files (initial and final) along with additional support materials for the book are available.

To obtain additional CSWP exam information and to take the free sample Segment 1 exam, visit https://3dexperience.virtualtester.com/#home

If your school is an academic certification provider, your instructor can allocate a free exam credit for the CSWP - Segment 1, Segment 2 or Segment 3. The instructor will require your .edu email address.

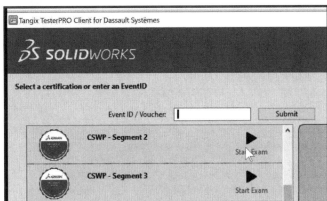

TABLE OF CONTENTS

TESTING TIPS

I have collected various testing tips over the years from my colleagues and friends on the SOLIDWORKS Certification exams. Below is a list that may help you prepare and pass the CSWP exam.

1. It is an exam. It is timed. There is no partial credit. Be precise in your work and entering your answers with the correct number of decimal places. Were you perfect in the sample CSWP exam or on the examples in this book? If not, why? Correct the mistakes before taking the real exam; you will be glad you did.

2. The sample CSWP exam only covers Segment 1 of the CSWP CORE exam. Time yourself on the practice exam. You should be able to finish the sample Segment 1 exam in approximately 50 minutes.

3. Read up on the contents of the exam that you are not familiar with (collision detection, interference detection, Advanced mates, measure tool, design tables, equations, global variables, coordinate locations, replace components, etc.) before you take any segment of the CSWP CORE exam.

4. You will be tested on data found in the Mass Properties section of SOLIDWORKS. It is important to be familiar with accessing Mass Properties and interpreting them correctly.

5. The second question in most segments is usually in a multiple-choice format. You need the exact answer (within .5% of the stated value) before you move on to the next question (fill in the blank). If you don't find your answer (within .5%) in the multiple-choice single answer format section, recheck your solid model for precision and accuracy.

6. In Segment 1 of the CSWP CORE exam use global variables A thru E. Use Equations for X & Y. This will save you time.

7. In Segment 1, change the label of the dimensions in your model to A, B, C, D, etc. to visually keep track of which dimensions need to be changed. As an alternative, you can also use the Design Table to manage the changing parameters.

8. Create a directory and file structure to save your model during the exam. Create a millimeter, 2 decimal place, part template and assembly template.

9. Take the test on a system you are familiar with. Don't customize your system right before you take the exam.

10. Read all questions before beginning. Pay attention to material changes, origin location, dimensional changes. Note which values indicated by a letter are the ones that will change.

11. Rely only on dimensions and provided information. Do NOT rely on the image provided as a template. Dimensions are changed from test to test so the image used will not be to scale (this is noted in the exam).

12. SOLIDWORKS displays a circle, ellipse or a square around the areas and features that require modification from the original part.

13. Notice where the dimensions are referenced in the drawing views. If the dimensions are referenced from the lower right-hand corner, this is where you should begin with the origin for your Base Sketch (Sketch1).

14. If you use faces versus a dimension, this can help when you need to create a design change to maintain the design intent of the part.

15. Suppress features before you delete them. This will inform you if there are any rebuild or feature errors during modification.

16. Always enter the needed decimal places in the answer field even if 0's. Example: 120.00.

17. Always confirm that your math is correct. Use the Measure tool.

18. As a general rule, insert relations before dimensions in a sketch.

19. Fillets and rounds are modified often in Segment 1. Use caution when taking the exam. Fillets and rounds are displayed in red.

20. Care should be used when you Copy and Paste to create new configurations. Repair all errors before you continue.

21. Utilize the split bar to work between the FeatureManager and the ConfigurationManager in Segment 2 of the CSWP CORE exam.

22. In Segment 3 of the CSWP CORE exam, the first component in the assembly should be fixed to the origin or fully defined.

23. You may be required to measure angles between flat surfaces. Be certain to understand the direction, complement or supplement of the required angle.

24. Confirm the position of components inside an assembly when using the Replace Components tool. Apply the Change Transparency tool or a section view to confirm mated component location.

25. SOLIDWORKS will provide a part to create that is not orientated correctly in the assembly. Knowledge of component orientation and changing orientation in an assembly is required along with creating a coordinate system.

26. Save your work frequently and rename saved parts in all segments of the exam.

27. Imported components have imported geometry. Select **NO** on Feature Recognition. Import the geometry as quickly as possible.

28. During the exam, utilize the various drawing view options and zoom tool to better understand the location of fillets and rounds. Fillets and rounds are displayed in red.

29. During the exam, it may state: Roll Control: Free. Pitch/Yaw Control: Free. This means you can rotate freely about X, Y, and Z in the assembly.

30. Relax. Exam anxiety can be a killer. Take a deep breath and enjoy.

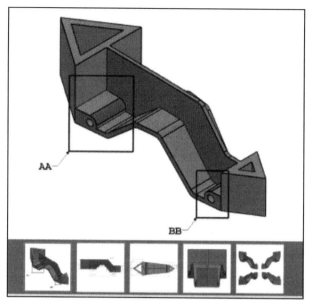

☀ There are numerous ways to build the models in this book. A goal is to display different design intents and techniques.

☀ If your school is an academic certification provider, your instructor can allocate a free exam credit (CSWP - Segment 1, CSWP Segment 2, or CSWP Segment 3). The instructor will require your .edu email address.

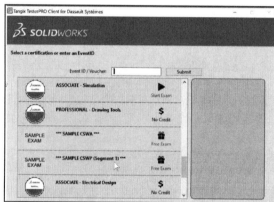

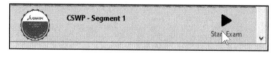

CHAPTER 1 - SEGMENT 1 OF THE CSWP CORE EXAM

Introduction

The CSWP Certification exam is offered in three separate segments. The three-segment exam allows you to take each segment at any time, and in any order. Once you pass a segment, you will not have to take it again.

Segment 1 is not a prerequisite for Segment 2, Segment 2 is not a prerequisite for Segment 3.

View the provided SOLIDWORKS CSWP Sample Exam folder. The folder contains a pdf with information on the following: exam details, how to prepare for the exam, how to take the practice exam, taking the exam (only for Segment 1), sample test quesitons, test answers, and helpful sites.

Visit https://3dexperience.virtualtester.com/#home to take the free online Sample CSWP (Segement 1) exam using the virtualtester. Create an account.

You need to wait 30 days before you can retake the free sample exam.

Download all needed model files (initial and final) and the SOLIDWORKS CSWP Sample Exam folder from the SDC Publications website (www.SDCpublications.com/downloads/978-1-63057-542-7).

⚡ If your school is an academic certification provider, your instructor can allocate a free exam credit for the CSWP (Segment 1, Segment 2 or Segment 3). The instructor will require your .edu email address.

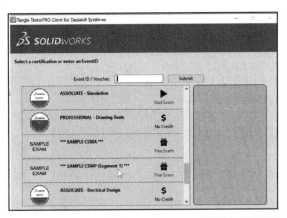

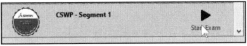

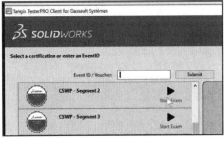

SOLIDWORKS Certification Exam Guide & Practice Test

PROFESSIONAL
Mechanical
Design

ƧS SOLIDWORKS

CSWP: Certified SOLIDWORKS Professional

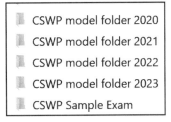

📁 CSWP model folder 2020
📁 CSWP model folder 2021
📁 CSWP model folder 2022
📁 CSWP model folder 2023
📁 CSWP Sample Exam

Taking the CSWP Segment 1 Exam

Go to the 3DEXPERIENCE® Certification Center at 3DEXPERIENCE® Certification Center (virtualtester.com).

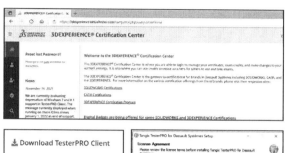

The 3DEXPERIENCE® Certification Center is where you are able to login to manage your certificates, take certifications, and make changes to your account settings.

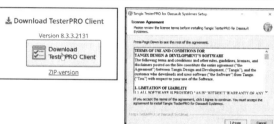

If your school is an academic certification provider, your instructor can allocate free exam credits.

The instructor will require your .edu email address.

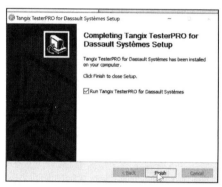

Download the TesterPRO Client.

Un-zip the Tester PRO Client.

Read the License Agreement. Agree to the Candidate Conduct Policy. Click I Agree.

Install the Tester PRO Client. Click install. Click Finish.

Select Test Language. Click Continue.

Create an account. If you already have an account, select "I already have a VirtulTester UserID and password".

Login. Click Continue.

Click SOLIDWORKS.

Select the CSWP Segment 1 exam. In this case, the instructor allocated the CSWP Segment 1 exam credit.

Click Start Exam.

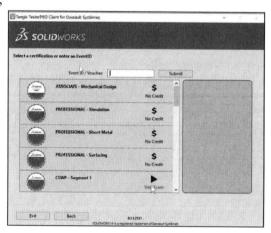

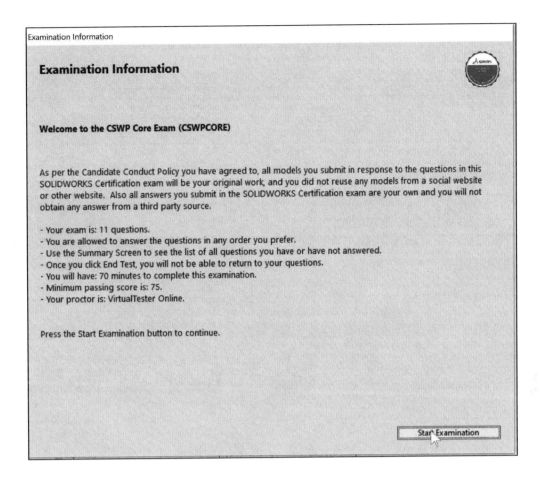

Segment 1 is 70 minutes long with eleven (11) questions.

A total score of 75 out of 105 or better is required to pass. All answers are in the MMGS unit standard. Decimal place 2.

In Segment 1, you will perform initial part creation, initial part update and various stage modifications.

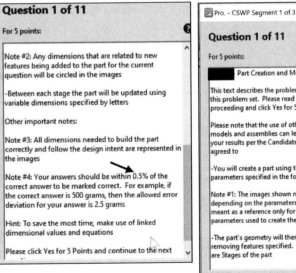

The format is either multiple-choice or single fill in the blank. The first question is an instructional page. Read the instructions. Agree to the Candidate Conduct Policy. Click Yes. It's a free 5 points.

The second question is a multiple-choice format.

You should have the exact answer (within .5% of the stated value in the multiple-choice section) before you move on to the next question. If you don't have the exact answer, you will most likely fail the following question. This is crucial as there is no partial credit.

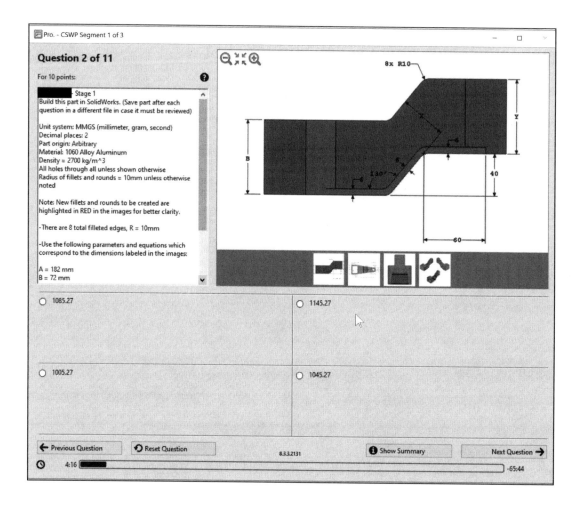

All holes are through all unless shown otherwise.

Parameters and or equations will change between questions.

Fillets and rounds are highlighted in RED during the exam for better clarity. There can be up to 8 fillets on a part.

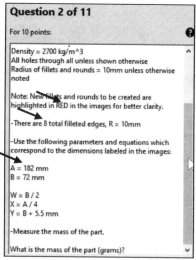

There are three major stages to be modeled: Stage 1 (question 2), Stage 2 (question 5) and Stage 3 (question 8).

Questions 3, 4, 6, 7, 9, 10, and 11 request the user to create modifications.

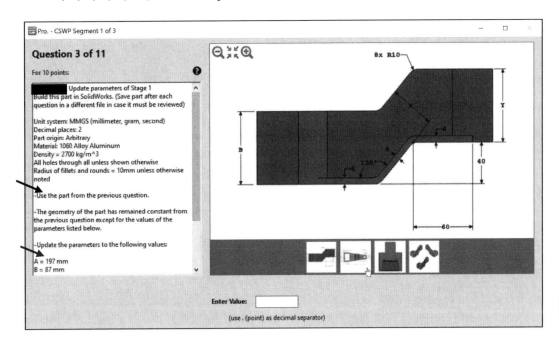

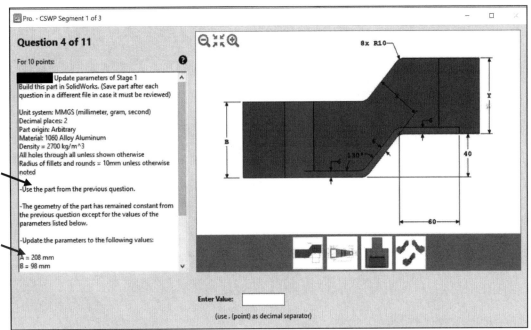

Strategically it is best if a user does questions 2, 5, and 8 to model the major stages and compare their Mass Properties to the multiple-choice answer.

You should be within .5% of the stated value in the multiple-choice section before you go back to questions 3, 4, 6, 7, 9, 10, and 11 (single fill in the blank format) to make the changes.

Engineering drawing views with annotations are presented to you in all segments of the CSWP exam.

During the exam, utilize the various drawing view options and zoom tool to better understand the location of fillets, rounds and dimensions.

The changes between parts in each question are concentrated in indicated areas as shown below with a box or circle.

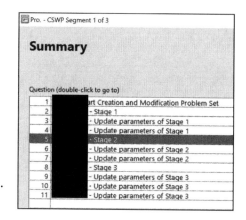

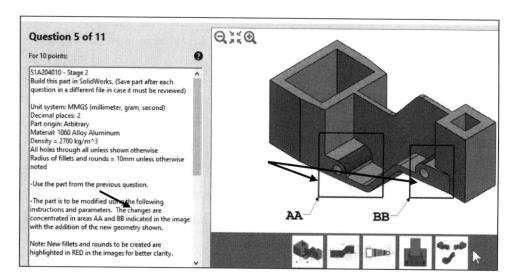

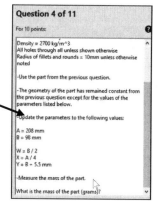

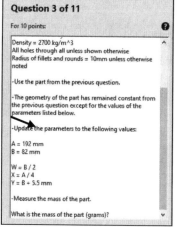

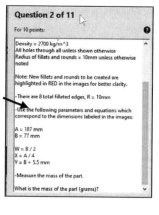

Read and understand an Engineering document

What is an Engineering document? In SOLIDWORKS a part, assembly, or drawing is referred to as a document. Each document is displayed in the Graphics window.

During the exam, each question will display an information table on the left side of the screen and drawing information on the right.

Read the provided information and apply it to the drawing. Various values are provided in each question.

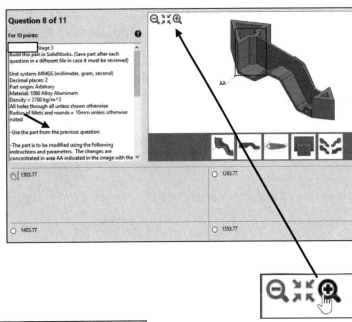

If you do not find your answer (within 0.5%) in the multiple choice single answer format section - recheck your solid model for precision and accuracy.

Use the magnifying glass tool during the exam to zoom in / out on the part or assembly views.

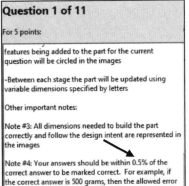

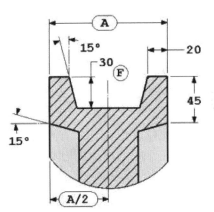

SOLIDWORKS views present illustrations that are not proportional to the given dimensions.

Engineering Documentation Practices

2D drawing views are displayed in the CSWP exam. The ability to interpret a 2D drawing view is required.

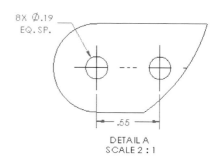

Example 1: *8X Ø.19 EQ. SP*. Eight holes with a .19in. diameter are required that are equally (.55in.) spaced.

Example 2: *R2.50 TYP*. Typical radius of 2.50. The dimension has a two decimal place precision.

Example 3: ⏚. The Depth/Deep ⏚ symbol with a 1.50 dimension associated with the hole. The hole Ø.562 has a three decimal place precision.

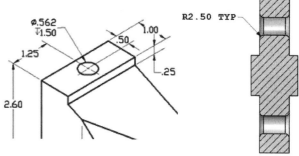

Example 4: *A+40*. A is provided to you on the exam. 44mm + A.

N is a Detail view of the M-M Section view.

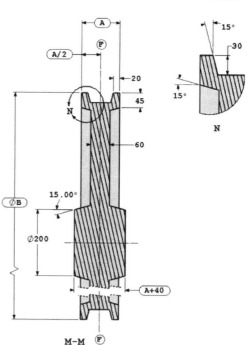

- Example 5: *ØB*. Diameter of B. B is provided to you on the exam.

- Example 6: ⏥. Parallelism.

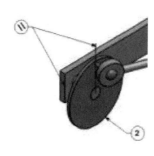

Build the part from the detailed illustrations

Segment 1 of the CSWP exam - First question

Below is the needed information and steps to correctly create the provided model in the sample CSWP segment 1 exam.

Provided Information:

Initial part - Stage 1: Build this part in SOLIDWORKS.

Unit system: MMGS (millimeter, gram, second)

Decimal places: 2

Part origin: Arbitrary

Material: Alloy Steel

Density: 0.0077 g/mm^3

All holes through all unless shown otherwise.

Use the following parameters and equations which correspond to the dimensions labeled in the images:

A = 213 mm

B = 200 mm

C = 170 mm

D = 130 mm

E = 41 mm

Test Questions

This section will give you a general idea of Segment 1 of the CSWP Exam. These images are to be used to answer Questions #1 - 3.

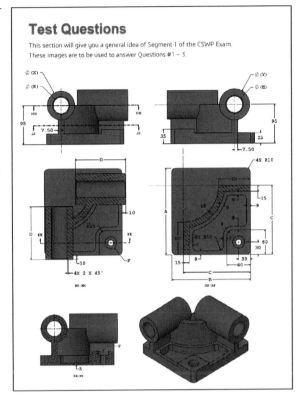

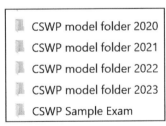

SOLIDWORKS Certification Exam Guide & Practice Test

PROFESSIONAL
Mechanical Design

S SOLIDWORKS

CSWP: Certified SOLIDWORKS Professional

CSWP model folder 2020
CSWP model folder 2021
CSWP model folder 2022
CSWP model folder 2023
CSWP Sample Exam

F = Hole Wizard Standard: ANSI Metric - Counterbore

Type: Hex Bolt - ANSI B18.2.3.5M

Size: M8

Fit: Close

Through Hole Diameter: 15.00 mm

Counterbore Diameter: 30.00 mm

Counterbore Depth: 10.00 mm

End Condition: Through All

X = A/3

Y = B/3 + 10mm

Hint #1: The dimensions that are to be linked or updated and are variable will be labeled with letters. Any dimensions that are simple value changes from one stage to another will be circled in the images.

Hint #2: To save the most time, make use of Global Variables "linked dimensional values" and equations.

Measure the mass of the part. Note: Depending on the SOLIDWORKS year, your answer may vary by .01%.

What is the mass of the part (grams)?

a) 14139.65

b) 14298.56

c) 15118.41

d) 14207.34

1. Stage 1 – Initial Part
Build this part in SOLIDWORKS

Unit system: MMGS (millimeter, gram, second)
Decimal places: 2
Part origin: Arbitrary
Material: Alloy Steel
Density = 0.0077 g/mm^3
All holes through all unless shown otherwise

Use the following parameters and equations which correspond to the dimensions labeled in the images:

A = 213 mm
B = 200 mm
C = 170 mm
D = 130 mm
E = 41 mm
F = Hole Wizard Standard: Ansi Metric Counterbore
    Type: Hex Bolt – ANSI B18.2.3.5M
    Size: M8
    Fit: Close
    Through Hole Diameter: 15.00 mm
    Counterbore Diameter: 30.00 mm
    Counterbore Depth: 10.00 mm
    End Condition: Through All
X = A/3
Y = B/3 + 10mm

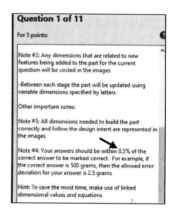

Question 1 of 11

For 5 points:

Note #2: Any dimensions that are related to new features being added to the part for the current question will be circled in the images

-Between each stage the part will be updated using variable dimensions specified by letters

Other important notes:

Note #3: All dimensions needed to build the part correctly and follow the design intent are represented in the images

Note #4: Your answers should be within 0.5% of the correct answer to be marked correct. For example, if the correct answer is 500 grams, then the allowed error deviation for your answer is 2.5 grams

Hint: To save the most time, make use of linked dimensional values and equations

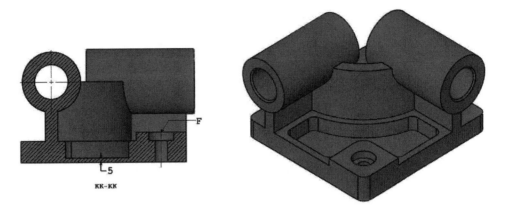

When you begin segment 1 of the CSWP, you will be presented with a variety of drawing views and parameters specified in the question. Take your time to first understand the provided drawing views. Then comprehend the provided geometry and geometric relations which are provided.

In the sample exam, the variables are (A, B, C, D, E & F). F is a Hole Wizard hole.

You will see anywhere between 5 to 6 variables and 2 equations in this segment of the exam.

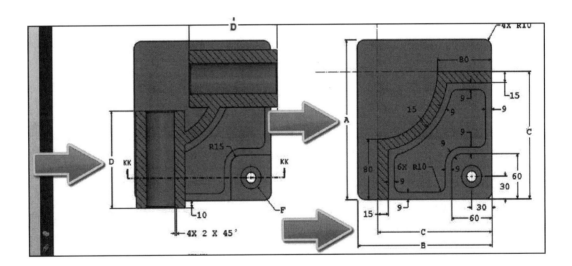

Observe where the dimensions are referenced. In the illustrated example, the dimensions are referenced from the lower right-hand corner. This is where you should begin with the origin of the rectangle for the Base Sketch (Sketch1) in this example.

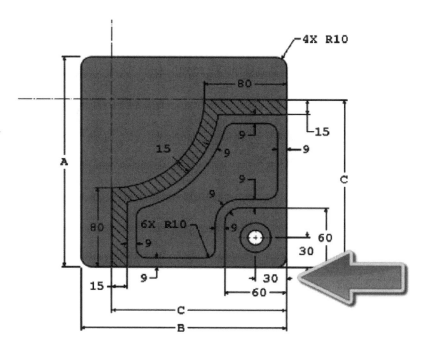

Most questions ask for a center of gravity or mass in grams. For the former it is crucial that the model is oriented exactly as illustrated. For the latter, it does not matter as much, but do not take the chance.

Global Variables can be used for many of the same purposes as linked values (also referred to as shared values or linked dimensions). Global Variables are much easier to find, change, and manage than linked values. A Global variable is just a name assigned to a dimension, a reference measurement, or an entire equation. Global Variables are assigned in the Equations dialog box or in the Modify dimension box as simply the variable name equaling an expression of a value.

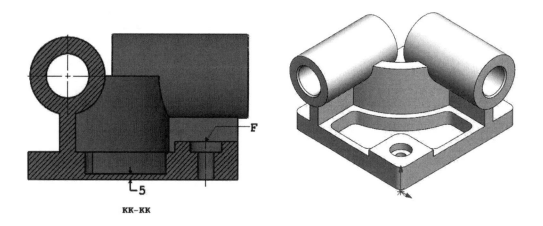

Be aware of what is symmetrical and what is different. The two cylinders look the same, but they are not. They have different diameters. It would not make sense to create a pattern or to mirror the two.

Look at the provided variables. Ask yourself, what requires a Global variable in the Equation folder to address speedy part modification in a timed exam?

Understand the provided Hole type.

Based on the provided information, create an Equation folder and input the variables.

SOLIDWORKS displays a circle, ellipse or a square around the areas and features that require modification from the original part.

Remember, the purpose of the book is not to educate a new or intermediate user on SOLIDWORKS, but to inform them on the types of questions, layout and what to expect when taking the three segments of the CSWP CORE exam.

In this section, address part modification through an Equation folder using Global Variables, equations or a design table.

Perform the procedure that you are the most comfortable with.

The Modify dialog box accepts equations. You can also use it to create on-the fly Global Variables. To start an equation in the Modify box, start by replacing the numeric value with an = sign in the value box. When you do this, you will see a drop-down menu for functions and file properties. Use the dimension entry box.

```
A = 213 mm
B = 200 mm
C = 170 mm
D = 130 mm
E = 41 mm
F = Hole Wizard Standard: Ansi Metric Counterbore
    Type: Hex Bolt – ANSI B18.2.3.5M
    Size: M8
    Fit: Close
    Through Hole Diameter: 15.00 mm
    Counterbore Diameter: 30.00 mm
    Counterbore Depth: 10.00 mm
    End Condition: Through All
X = A/3
Y = B/3 + 10mm
```

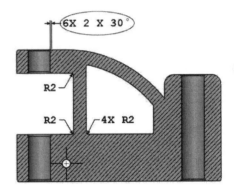

W-W

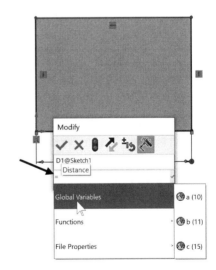

Let's begin.

1. **Create** a folder to save your models.

2. **Create** a new part.

3. **Set** document properties (drafting standard (ANSI), units (MMGS) and precision (2) for the model.

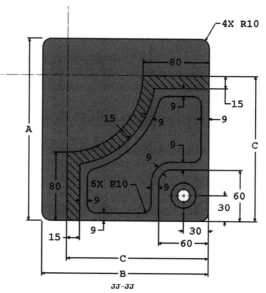

Start with setting the Global Variables. The provided variables are:

A = 213 mm

B = 200 mm

C = 170 mm

D = 130 mm

E = 41 mm

4. **Display** the Equation folder in the FeatureManager.

5. **Display** the Equations, Global Variables, and Dimension dialog box.

6. **Enter** the five Global Variables (A, B, C, D, & E) as illustrated.

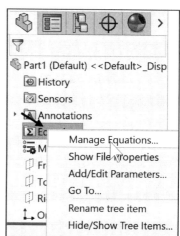

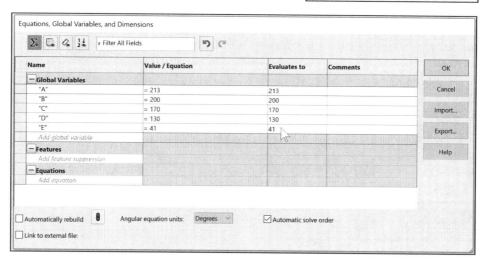

7. **Exit** the dialog box.

View the created Global Variables.

8. **Expand** the Equation folder in the FeatureManager.

Create the Base Sketch.

9. **Create** Sketch1. Select the Top Plane as the Sketch plane. Sketch1 is the profile for the Extruded Base (Boss-Extrude1) feature. Apply the Corner Rectangle Sketch tool. Click the origin and a position in the upper left section of the Graphics window. Most of the dimensions in the provided drawing view are referenced from this location.

10. **Insert** the horizontal dimension using the Global Variable B(200) from the Modify dialog box. Enter an equal sign (=) first in the Modify dialog box.

11. **Enter** B for Dimension Text. This will help you keep track of the variables.

12. **Insert** the vertical dimension using the Global Variable Λ(213) from the Modify dialog box. Sketch1 is fully defined.

13. **Enter** A for Dimension Text.

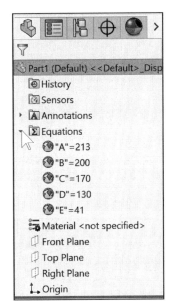

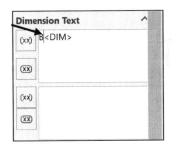

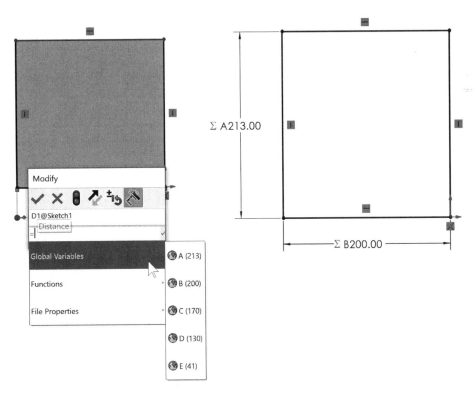

14. **Display** Primary values. Click View Dimension Names from the Heads-up toolbar. View the results in the Graphics window.

15. **Create** the Extruded Base feature. Boss-Extrude1 is the Base feature. Blind is the default End Condition in Direction 1. Depth = 25mm. Direction up.

16. **Assign** Alloy Steel material to the part.

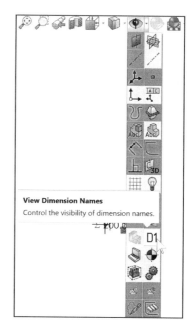

View Dimension Names
Control the visibility of dimension names.

Create the Extrude-Thin feature. The Extrude-Thin feature is controlled by the variable C and two dimensions that are equal (80mm). The height of the feature from the bottom is 95mm.

Start from the Top face and subtract 25mm from 95mm to obtain the correct depth for the Thin-Extrude feature.

17. **Create** Sketch2. Select the Top face. Sketch2 is the profile for the Extrude-Thin feature. Utilize the Line Sketch tool to create a vertical and horizontal line. Utilize the 3 Point Arc Sketch tool to complete the sketch.

18. **Add** an Equal relation between the vertical and horizontal line of Sketch2.

19. **Insert** the 80mm dimension on the vertical line.

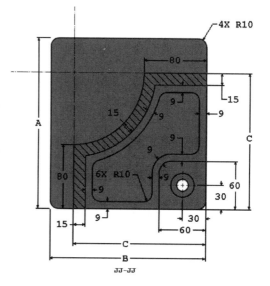

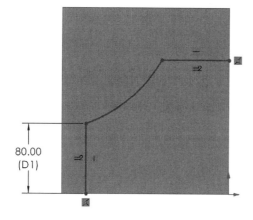

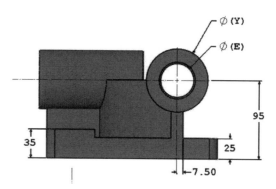

20. **Insert** the horizontal Global Variable C dimension as illustrated.

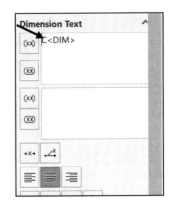

21. **Enter** C for Dimension Text.

22. **Insert** the vertical Global Variable C dimension.

23. **Enter** C for Dimension Text.

24. **Insert** a horizontal relation between the centerpoint of the arc and the horizontal sketch line end point if needed. The sketch is fully defined and is displayed in black.

25. **Insert** the Extrude-Thin feature. The Extrude-Thin feature is controlled by the Global Variable C and two dimensions that are equal (80mm). The overall height of the part is 95mm. Start from the Top face. Subtract 25mm from 95mm to obtain the correct depth for the Thin-Extrude feature. Click No in the Close Sketch With Model Edges dialog box. You want an open profile. If needed click the Reverse Direction in the Thin Feature box. Enter 15mm for Thickness. Enter 70mm for Depth in the Direction 1 box. Blind is the default End Conditions. Click OK from the Boss-Extrude PropertyManager. Extrude-Thin1 is displayed in the FeatureManager.

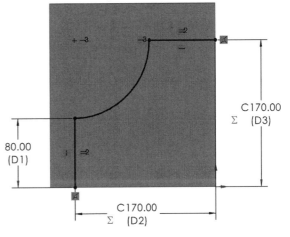

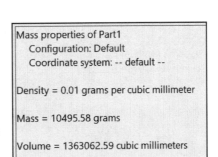

At this time, your model should have a mass of **10495.58 grams**. You should have the exact answer (within .5% of the stated value in the multiple choice section) before you move on to the next question.

Mass properties of Part1
  Configuration: Default
  Coordinate system: -- default --

Density = 0.01 grams per cubic millimeter

Mass = 10495.58 grams

Volume = 1363062.59 cubic millimeters

Create the first cylinder, (remember the two cylinders are not the same). The first cylinder outside diameter is controlled by equation X. X = A/3. The inside diameter is E = (41mm) and the depth is D = (130mm).

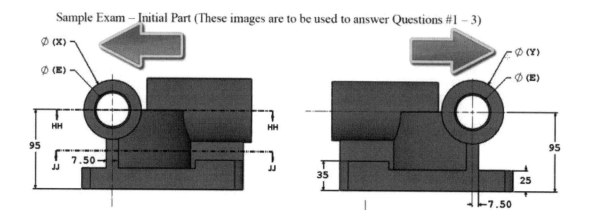

Sample Exam – Initial Part (These images are to be used to answer Questions #1 – 3)

The first cylinder is offset 10mm from the Front Plane or face.

26. **Create** a Plane offset from the Front Plane (front face) 10mm. Plane1 is created.

27. **Create** Sketch3 on Plane1. Sketch a circle with the centerpoint, Coincident at the midpoint of the Extrude-Thin1 feature. The dimension is driven by the X equation.

28. **Enter** the equation for X in the Modify dialog box.

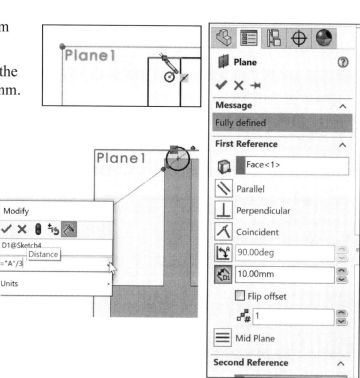

29. **Create** the Extruded Boss feature from Sketch3. Enter the extruded distance of the Global Variable D. Depth D = 130mm. Click Reverse direction if needed.

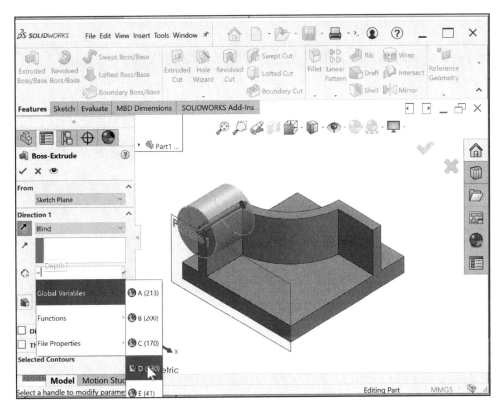

30. **View** the results in the Graphics window.

🔆 There are numerous ways to build the model in this section. A goal is to display different design intents and techniques.

🔆 Depending on the SOLIDWORKS year, your answer may vary by .01%.

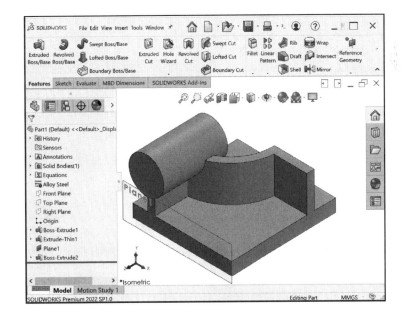

31. **Create** Sketch4 on the front face of the cylinder to create the Extruded Cut feature. Use the Circle Sketch tool. Click the centerpoint of the Extruded Boss feature for the centerpoint.

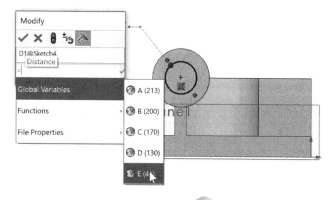

32. **Dimension** Sketch4. Insert the Global Variable E. E = 41mm.

33. **Enter** E for Dimension Text.

34. **Create** an Extruded Cut feature using Sketch4. Select Through All for End Condition to address any future design change for depth.

At this time, your model should have a mass of **12722.39 grams**. You should have the exact answer (within 0.5% of the stated value in the multiple choice section) before you move on to the next question.

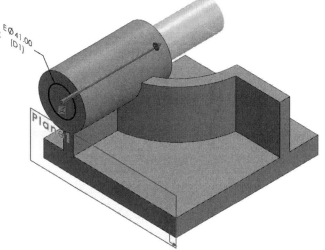

Create the second cylinder (remember the two cylinders are _not_ the same).

The second cylinder outside diameter is controlled by equation Y.

Y = B/3 +10mm.

The inside diameter is E = (41mm).

The depth is D = (130mm).

Mass properties of Part1
    Configuration: Default
    Coordinate system: -- default --

Density = 0.01 grams per cubic millimeter

Mass = 12722.39 grams

Volume = 1652258.61 cubic millimeters

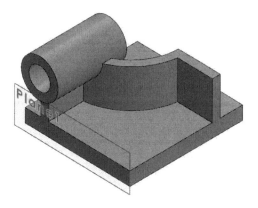

The second cylinder is offset 10mm from either the Right Plane or right face.

35. **Create** a Plane (Plane2) offset from the Right Plane (right face) 10mm.

36. **Create** Sketch5 on Plane2. Sketch a circle with the centerpoint Coincident at the midpoint of the Extrude-Thin1 feature. The dimension is driven by the Y equation.

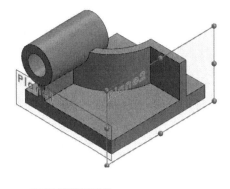

37. **Dimension** Sketch5. Enter the equation for Y in the Modify dialog box as displayed.

38. **Create** the Extruded Boss feature from Sketch5. Enter the extruded distance of the Global Variable D. Depth D = 130mm. Click Reverse direction if needed.

39. **View** the results in the Graphics window.

40. **Save** the part.

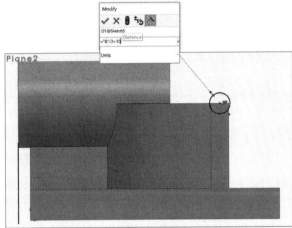

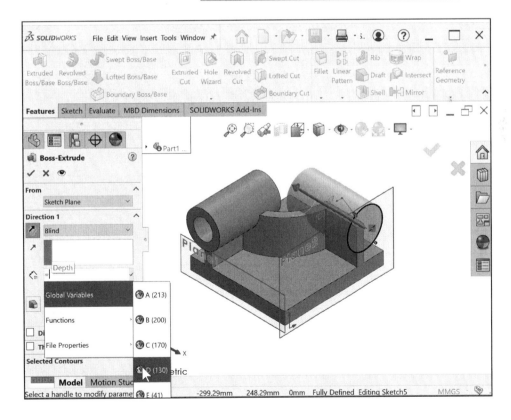

41. Create the Extruded Cut. **Create** Sketch6 on the Right face of the second cylinder. Use the Circle Sketch tool. Click the centerpoint of the Extruded Boss feature for the centerpoint.

42. **Insert** the Global Variable E. E = 41mm.

43. **Enter** E for Dimension Text.

44. **Create** an Extruded Cut feature from Sketch6. Select Through All for End Condition to address any future design change in depth.

At this time, your model should have a mass of **15562.83 grams**.

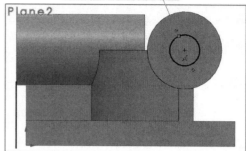

Always enter the needed decimal places in the answer field.

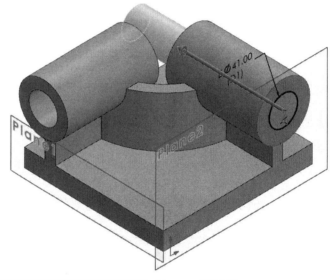

Mass properties of Part1
    Configuration: Default
    Coordinate system: -- default --

Density = 0.01 grams per cubic millimeter

Mass = 15562.82 grams

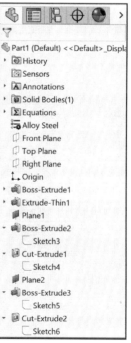

Create the Extruded Boss, Counterbore, and Fillet features on the right side of the model. Note: Fillets and rounds are displayed in red on the exam.

45. **Create** Sketch7 on the top face of Boss-Extrude1. Apply the Corner Rectangle tool from the right-hand side. Insert Equal geometric relations. Enter 60mm for dimension.

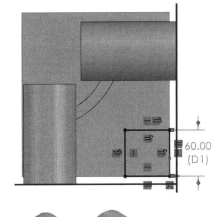

46. **Create** Boss-Extrude4 from Sketch7. Depth = 10mm. (35mm - 25mm) = 10mm from the provided information in the question.

Create the Counterbore hole using the Hole Wizard feature tool. Remember the provided information.

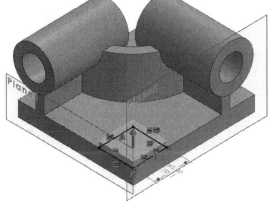

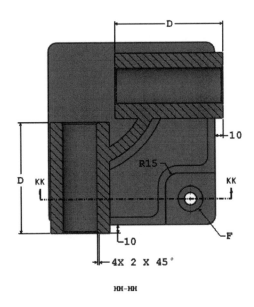

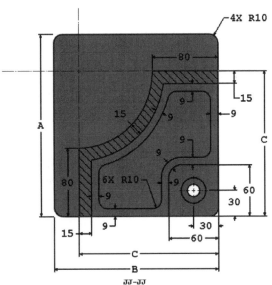

47. **Create** the Counterbore hole using the Hole Wizard on the top face of Boss-Extrude4.

There are numerous ways to build the models in this chapter. A goal is to display different design intents and techniques.

48. **Enter** the provided information in the Hole Specification PropertyManager. This is a Through All End Condition hole.

49. **Create** Sketch8. Use the Centerline Sketch tool with a Midpoint relation to locate the center of the hole on the Boss-Extrude4 face. This saves time from creating two dimensions. The hole is complete.

50. **Create** the first Constant radius Fillet (15mm) on the inside corner of the Boss-Extrude4 feature. You can use the Multiple radius fillet option to create all needed fillets, but for design intent and future modifications in the exam, insert two separate fillet features.

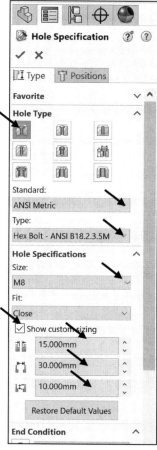

Use caution when taking the CSWP exam. Fillets are created and modified often.

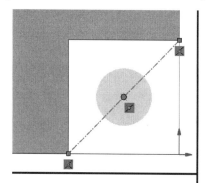

51. **Create** the second Constant radius Fillet (10mm) on the four outside edges of Boss-Extrude1.

At this time, your model should have a mass of **15729.68 grams**.

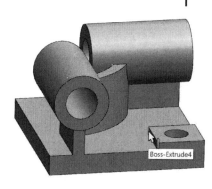

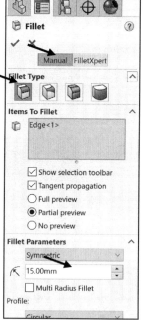

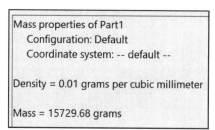

Mass properties of Part1
   Configuration: Default
   Coordinate system: -- default --

Density = 0.01 grams per cubic millimeter

Mass = 15729.68 grams

Create the Extruded Cut feature (pocket) on the top face of Boss-Extrude1 using the Offset Entities Sketch tool; then create the Chamfer feature.

52. **Create** Sketch10. Use the Offset Entities Sketch (9mm Offset distance) tool. Note the direction of the offset.

53. **Create** the Cut-Extrude3 feature based on the bottom face of the model. Utilize the Offset from Surface End Condition. Enter 5mm from the provided model information.

At this time, your model should have a mass of **14198.79** grams.

If you use faces vs. dimensions when creating features, this can help when you need to create a design change to maintain the design intent of the part.

54. **Insert** six (6) Constant radius Fillet features (10mm) on the Cut-Extrude3 feature per the provided information. Fillet3 is created.

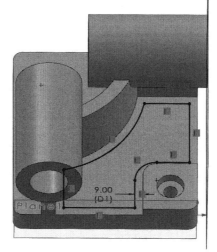

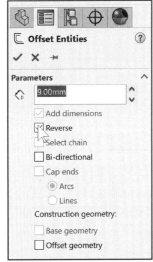

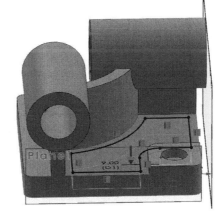

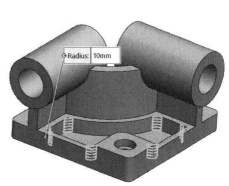

Insert the last feature for the part, Chamfer1.

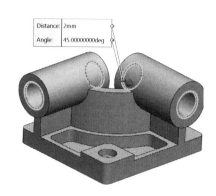

55. **Create** a Chamfer (Angle Distance) feature on the internal diameter edges of the cylinders. Angle = 45. Distance = 2mm. Select four edges. The last 2 edges are on the back of the cylinder.

56. **Calculate** the Mass Properties. Note: Depending on the SOLIDWORKS year, your answer may vary by .01%.

57. **Select 14207.34** grams for the answer in this section. The number matches the answer of d. You should be within .5% of the stated value before you move to the next section to modify the original part.

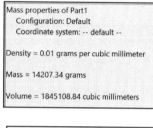

58. **Save** the part.

59. **Save as a copy Part2** for the second question. You are finished with this section.

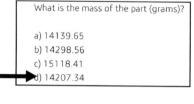

Always enter the needed decimal places in the answer field.

This section presents a representation of the types of questions that you will see in this segment of the exam.

Always save your models to verify the results.

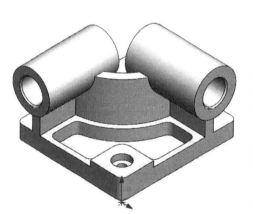

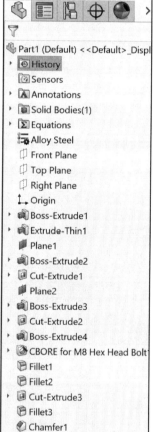

Segment 1 of the CSWP CORE exam - Second question

In this section, modify the original part using Global Variables . The material and units are the same but the variables A thru E are different from their original values.

The Hole Wizard feature remains the same and the equation X and Y remain the same from the original part.

Read the question carefully. This section provides a single fill in the blank format, not a multiple choice format.

Provided Information: Update parameters of the initial part.

Unit system: MMGS (millimeter, gram, second)

Decimal places: 2

Part origin: Arbitrary

Material: Alloy Steel

Density: 0.0077 g/mm^3

All holes through all unless shown otherwise.

Use the following parameters and equations which correspond to the dimensions labeled in the images:

A = 225 mm

B = 210 mm

C = 176 mm

D = 137 mm

E = 39 mm

F = Hole Wizard Standard: ANSI Metric - Counterbore

   Type: Hex Bolt - ANSI B18.2.3.5M

   Size: M8

   Fit: Close

   Through Hole Diameter: 15.00 mm

   Diameter: 30.00 mm

   Counterbore Depth: 10.00 mm

   End Condition: Through All

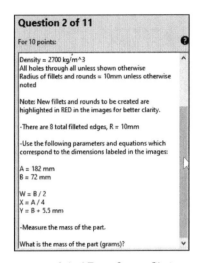

Actual Exam Screen Shot

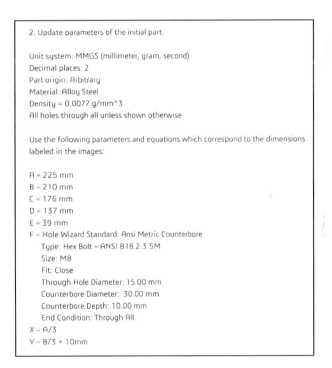

X = A/3

Y = B/3 + 10mm

Hint #1: The dimensions that are to be linked or updated and are variable will be labeled with letters. Any dimensions that are simple value changes from one stage to another will be circled in the images.

Hint #2: To save the most time, make use of linked dimensional values and equations.

Measure the mass of the part.

What is the mass of the part (grams)?

SOLIDWORKS displays a circle, ellipse or a square around the areas and features that require modification from the original part.

🔆 The images displayed on the exam are not to scale due to differences in the parts being downloaded for each tester.

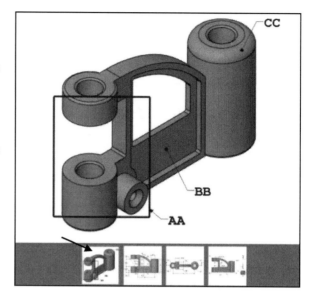

Actual Exam Screen Shots

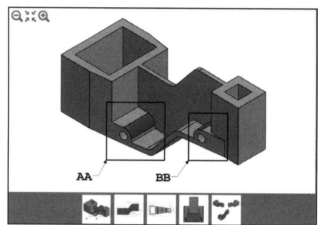

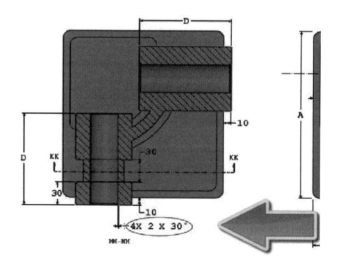

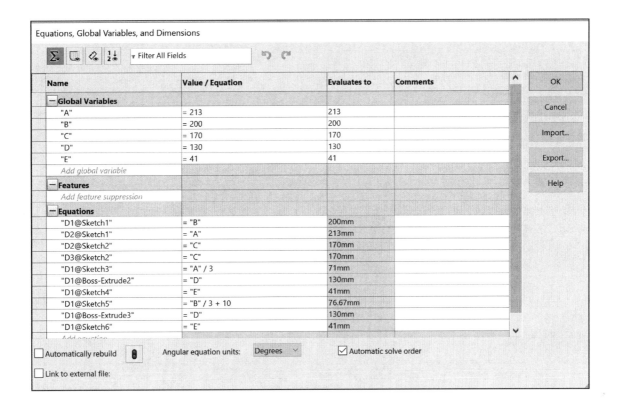

Let's begin.

Modify the variables that are different from Part1.

1. **Display** the Equations, Global Variables, and Dimensions dialog box.

2. **Enter** the five new Global Variables (A, B, C, D, & E) as illustrated.

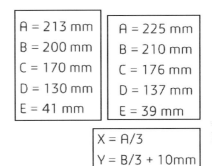

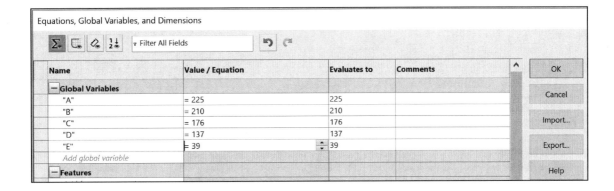

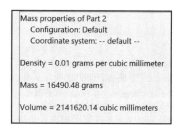

Mass properties of Part 2
  Configuration: Default
  Coordinate system: -- default --

Density = 0.01 grams per cubic millimeter

Mass = 16490.48 grams

Volume = 2141620.14 cubic millimeters

🔅 Double-click on a feature to modify the Global Variable.

3. **Calculate** the mass of the model in grams.

4. **Enter 16490.48** grams. Depending on the SOLIDWORKS year, your answer may vary by .01%.

5. **Save** the part.

6. **Save as a copy Part3** for the third question of the exam.

🔅 Always enter the needed decimal places in the answer field.

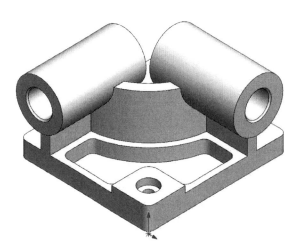

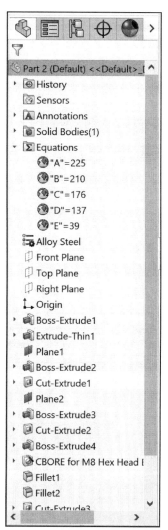

Segment 1 of the CSWP CORE exam - Third question

Update various parameters of the part. Modify the dimensions under Global Variables. Read the question carefully. Identify what variables and equations are the same vs. different. Has the material changed? Did a feature change? A question will be presented to you in multiple steps and you need to get each step correct to get the question correct.

Provided Information: Update parameters of the initial part.

Unit system: MMGS (millimeter, gram, second)

Decimal places: 2

Part origin: Arbitrary

Material: Alloy Steel

Density: 0.0077 g/mm^3

All holes through all unless shown otherwise.

Use the following parameters and equations which correspond to the dimensions labeled in the images:

A = 209 mm

B = 218 mm

C = 169 mm

D = 125 mm

E = 41 mm

F = Hole Wizard Standard: ANSI Metric - Counterbore

   Type: Hex Bolt - ANSI B18.2.3.5M

   Size: M8

   Fit: Close

   Through Hole Diameter: 15.00 mm

   Counterbore Diameter: 30.00 mm

   Counterbore Depth: 10.00 mm

   End Condition: Through All

X = A/3

Y = B/3 + 10mm

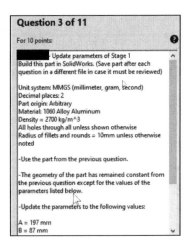

Question 3 of 11

For 10 points:

- Update parameters of Stage 1
Build this part in SolidWorks. (Save part after each question in a different file in case it must be reviewed)

Unit system: MMGS (millimeter, gram, second)
Decimal places: 2
Part origin: Arbitrary
Material: 1060 Alloy Aluminum
Density = 2700 kg/m^3
All holes through all unless shown otherwise
Radius of fillets and rounds = 10mm unless otherwise noted

-Use the part from the previous question.

-The geometry of the part has remained constant from the previous question except for the values of the parameters listed below.

-Update the parameters to the following values:

A = 197 mm
B = 87 mm

Actual Exam Screen Shot

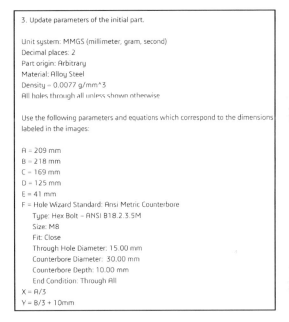

3. Update parameters of the initial part.

Unit system: MMGS (millimeter, gram, second)
Decimal places: 2
Part origin: Arbitrary
Material: Alloy Steel
Density – 0.0077 g/mm^3
All holes through all unless shown otherwise

Use the following parameters and equations which correspond to the dimensions labeled in the images:

A = 209 mm
B = 218 mm
C = 169 mm
D = 125 mm
E = 41 mm
F = Hole Wizard Standard: Ansi Metric Counterbore
     Type: Hex Bolt – ANSI B18.2.3.5M
     Size: M8
     Fit: Close
     Through Hole Diameter: 15.00 mm
     Counterbore Diameter: 30.00 mm
     Counterbore Depth: 10.00 mm
     End Condition: Through All
X = A/3
Y = B/3 + 10mm

Hint #1: The dimensions that are to be linked or updated and are variable will be labeled with letters. Any dimensions that are simple value changes from one stage to another will be circled in the images.

Hint #2: To save the most time, make use of Global Variables and equations.

Measure the mass of the part.

What is the mass of the part (grams)?

To display all dimensions, right-click Annotations folder from the FeatureManager and check the Display Annotations box.

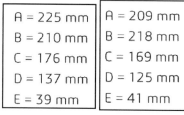

Let's begin.

1. **Display** the Equations, Global Variables, and Dimension dialog box.

2. **Enter** the five Global Variables (A, B, C, D, & E) as illustrated. Modify the variables that are different.

The equations ($X = A/3$, $Y = B/3 + 10$mm) have not been modified between the first, second or third question.

Segment 1 provides variables that either increase or decrease from the original part question. Design for this during the exam.

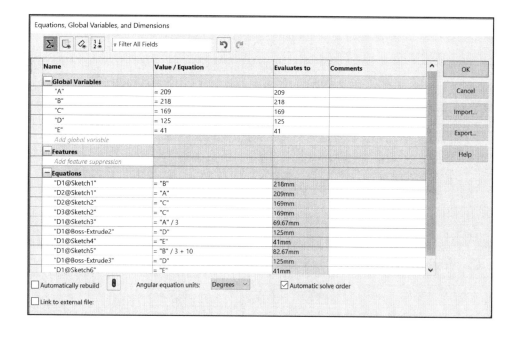

3. **Calculate** the mass of the model in grams.

4. **Enter 15100.46** grams.

5. **Save** the part.

6. **Rename** Part3 to Part4 for the fourth question of the exam.

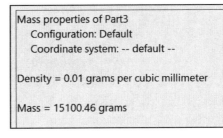

Mass properties of Part3
   Configuration: Default
   Coordinate system: -- default --

Density = 0.01 grams per cubic millimeter

Mass = 15100.46 grams

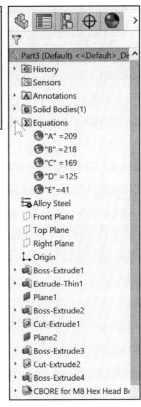

 Enter the needed decimal places in the answer field.

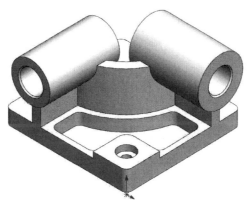

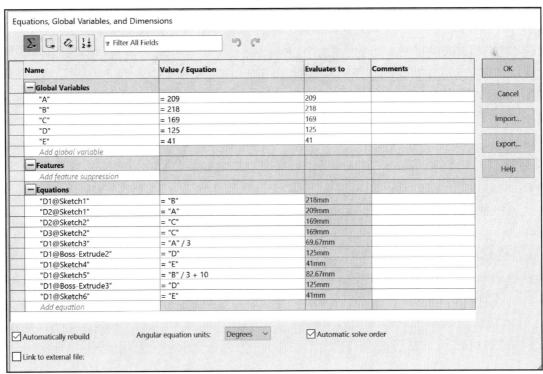

Equations, Global Variables, and Dimensions

Name	Value / Equation	Evaluates to	Comments
Global Variables			
"A"	= 209	209	
"B"	= 218	218	
"C"	= 169	169	
"D"	= 125	125	
"E"	= 41	41	
Add global variable			
Features			
Add feature suppression			
Equations			
"D1@Sketch1"	= "B"	218mm	
"D2@Sketch1"	= "A"	209mm	
"D2@Sketch2"	= "C"	169mm	
"D3@Sketch2"	= "C"	169mm	
"D1@Sketch3"	= "A" / 3	69.67mm	
"D1@Boss-Extrude2"	= "D"	125mm	
"D1@Sketch4"	= "E"	41mm	
"D1@Sketch5"	= "B" / 3 + 10	82.67mm	
"D1@Boss-Extrude3"	= "D"	125mm	
"D1@Sketch6"	= "E"	41mm	
Add equation			

☑ Automatically rebuild   Angular equation units: Degrees   ☑ Automatic solve order

☐ Link to external file:

OK Cancel Import... Export... Help

Segment 1 of the CSWP CORE exam - Fourth question

Stage 2: Modify the part using the following dimensions. (These images are to be used to answer questions 4 and 5.)

The changes from the initial part are concentrated in areas AA, BB, and CC shown in the first two images.

The needed modifications AA, BB, and CC are displayed with a circle, ellipse or a square in the exam.

Compare the information with your existing part. This question provides a multiple choice answer.

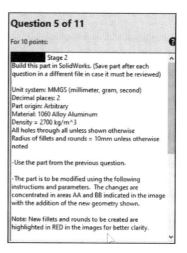

Question 5 of 11

For 10 points:

Stage 2
Build this part in SolidWorks. (Save part after each question in a different file in case it must be reviewed)

Unit system: MMGS (millimeter, gram, second)
Decimal places: 2
Part origin: Arbitrary
Material: 1060 Alloy Aluminum
Density = 2700 kg/m^3
All holes through all unless shown otherwise
Radius of fillets and rounds = 10mm unless otherwise noted

-Use the part from the previous question.

-The part is to be modified using the following instructions and parameters. The changes are concentrated in areas AA and BB indicated in the image with the addition of the new geometry shown.

Note: New fillets and rounds to be created are highlighted in RED in the images for better clarity.

Actual Exam Screen Shot

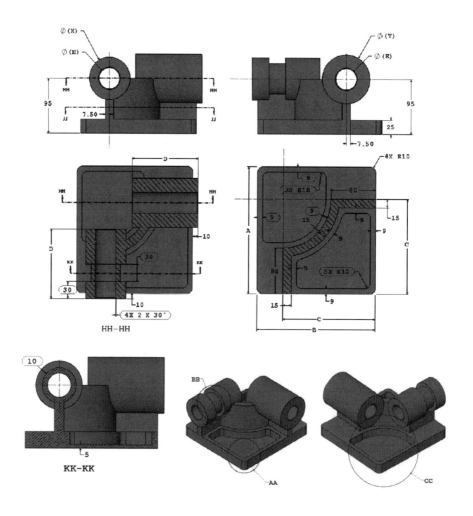

Provided Information:

4. Stage 2 - Modify

Modify the part using the following dimensions.

Unit system: MMGS (millimeter, gram, second)

Decimal places: 2

Part origin: Arbitrary

Material: Alloy Steel

Density: 0.0077 g/mm^3

All holes through all unless shown otherwise.

Use the following parameters and equations which correspond to the dimensions labeled in the images:

A = 221 mm

B = 211 mm

C = 165 mm

D = 121 mm

E = 37 mm

X = A/3

Y = B/3 + 15mm

Note: The equation for Y has changed from the initial part.

Hint #1: The dimensions that are to be linked or updated and are variable will be labeled with letters. Any dimensions that are simple value changes from one stage to another will be circled in the images.

Hint #2: To save the most time, make use of Global Variables and equations.

Measure the mass of the part.

What is the mass of the part (grams)?

a) 13095.40

b) 13206.40

c) 13313.35

d) 13395.79

4. Stage 2 – Modify

Modify the part using the following dimensions.

Note: The changes from the initial part are concentrated in areas AA, BB and CC shown in the images.

Unit system: MMGS (millimeter, gram, second)
Decimal places: 2
Part origin: Arbitrary
Material: Alloy Steel
Density = 0.0077 g/mm^3
All holes through all unless shown otherwise

Use the following parameters and equations which correspond to the dimensions labeled in the images:

A = 221 mm
B = 211 mm
C = 165 mm
D = 121 mm
E = 37 mm
X = A/3
Y = B/3 + 15mm

Note: The equation for Y has changed from the initial part.

The material and units are the same. Equation A is the same. Variables A thru E are different. The Hole Wizard feature is removed with a few other features as illustrated. Equation Y is different. Read the question carefully.

Address AA modification in the model. Create a single pocket and remove the Hole Wizard feature along with the Boss-Extrude4 feature and a few fillets. Recover and repair from missing items.

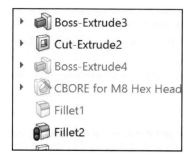

Let's begin.

1. **Suppress** Fillet1, CBORE and Boss-Extrude4. A dialog box is displayed.

2. **Press** the Stop and Repair button from the SOLIDWORKS dialog box. Fillet3 has a reference issue. There are missing items in the existing feature.

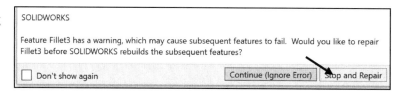

As a general rule, suppress features before you delete them. This will inform you if there are any rebuild or feature errors during modification in the exam.

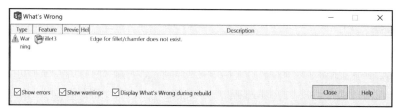

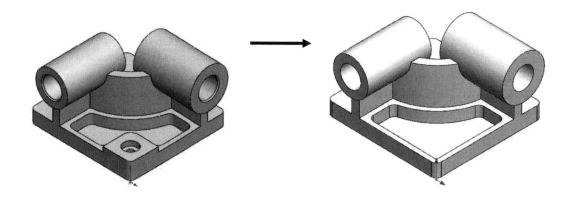

3. **Edit** the Fillet3 feature and repair. Delete any missing edges.

But wait, you can't insert the new edge (as illustrated) because it is part of the offset from the original sketch when you created the part.

Create a square corner for Sketch10 to select the needed edge for Fillet3.

4. **Edit** Sketch10 from the Cut-Extrude3 feature. Delete the fillet.

5. **Insert** the needed edge for Fillet3 using the Trim Entities sketch tool (Corner option).

6. **Edit** the Fillet3 feature and add the needed edge that you just created. Verify that you have 5 fillets with the radius of 10mm. There are no errors displayed in the FeatureManager.

7. **Delete** all suppressed features and any unneeded sketch in the FeatureManager: Fillet1, CBORE, Boss-Extrude4 and Sketch7. Suppress features before you delete them. This will inform you if there are any rebuild or feature errors during modification in the exam.

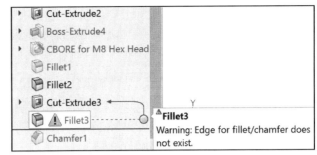

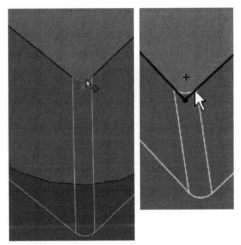

8. **Roll** back the Rollback bar in the FeatureManager. Your mass at this time should be **14378.42 grams**.

You should have the exact answer (within 0.5% of the stated value in the multiple choice section) before you move on to the next question.

9. **Save** the part.

Mass properties of Part4A
    Configuration: Default
    Coordinate system: -- default --

Density = 0.01 grams per cubic millimeter

Mass = 14378.42 grams

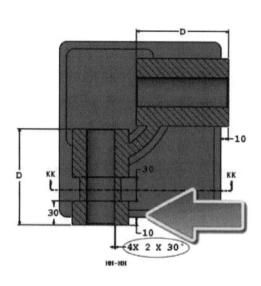

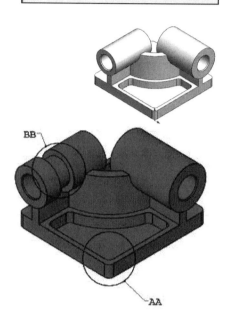

Address the BB modification in the model. Create a circular cut as illustrated on the left cylinder. The circular cut is offset 30mm from the front face of the cylinder. The depth of the cut is 30mm.

From the front view, the circular cut is offset 10mm and the circular cut does not go completely through the Extrude-Thin1 feature.

Then modify the Chamfer feature of the cylinders.

In this section utilize the Offset Entities, Convert Entities, Line and Trim Sketch tools to create the Base Sketch for the Extruded Cut feature.

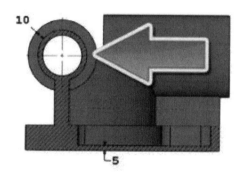

Let's begin.

10. **Create** a Sketch plane (30mm) offset from the front face of the cylinder as illustrated. Plane3 is displayed in the FeatureManager.

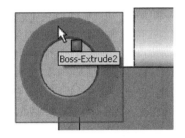
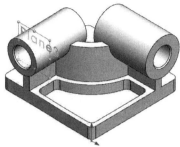

11. **Create** the Base Sketch on Plane3. Apply the Convert Entities Sketch tool to utilize the outside cylindrical geometry of the tube.

12. **Apply** the Offset Entities Sketch tool with an offset distance of 10mm. Click the outside cylindrical edge and reverse the direction if needed. You created an inside and outside ring for the Extruded Cut feature on your Base Sketch (Sketch11).

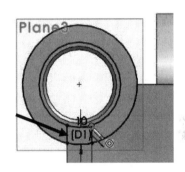

13. **Create** two vertical lines from the outside cylindrical edge to the inside cylindrical edge of the ring. The sketch is fully defined.

14. **Trim** any unwanted sketch geometry to finish the sketch for the Extruded Cut feature. Your Base sketch should consist of two arcs and two vertical lines.

15. **Create** an Extruded Cut feature with a depth of 30mm. The Extruded Cut feature removes the needed material and keeps the Extrude-Thin1 feature unbroken.

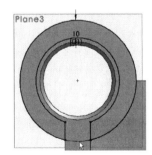

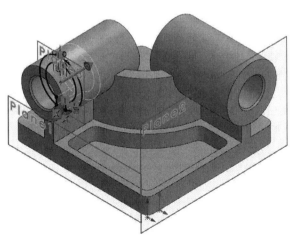

Next address the modification of the Chamfer feature in the front face of the cylinder.

16. **Modify** the cylinder Chamfer feature from 45 degrees to 30 degrees.

At this time your model should have a mass of **13983.95 grams**.

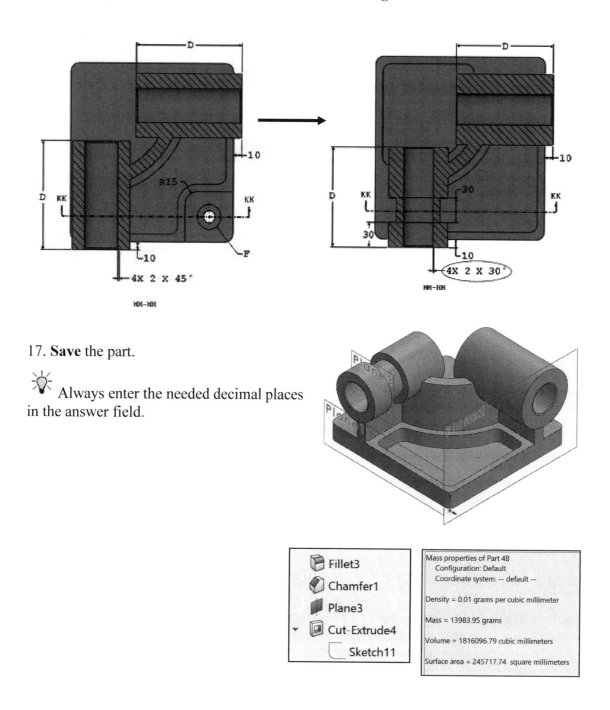

17. **Save** the part.

Always enter the needed decimal places in the answer field.

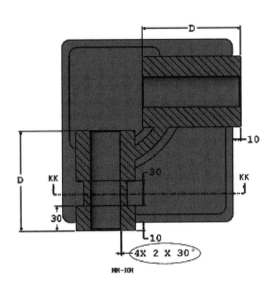

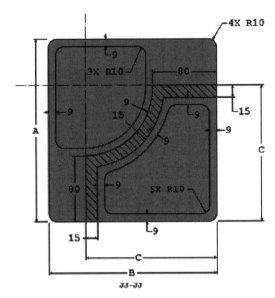

Address the Extruded Cut and fillet feature and then address the Global Variables A thru E and equation Y.

There are numerous ways to create the sketch for the Extruded Cut feature. In this case, utilize Construction geometry. Construction geometry helps you create a sketch but is not part of the feature.

18. **Create** a sketch using the Offset Entities Sketch tool on the top back face. Enter 9mm for Offset distance. Reverse the direction if needed.

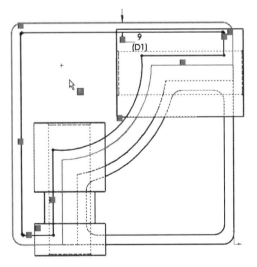

19. **Window-select** the part. Check the For construction box. Again, construction geometry helps create a sketch but is not part of the feature.

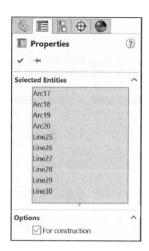

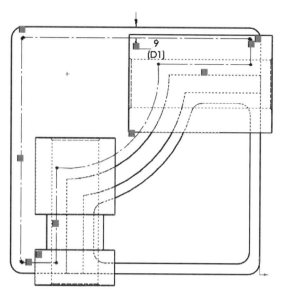

Create a 90⁰ Arc and inference the vertical line from the Extrude-Thin1 feature.

20. **Create** a 90⁰ Arc. Use the Centerpoint Arc Sketch tool. Click the centerpoint as illustrated, drag directly to the right until you see the inference symbol on the construction arc. Click the start point. Drag downward and click the end point to create the 90⁰ Arc. The mouse pointer displays A = 90 for angle feedback.

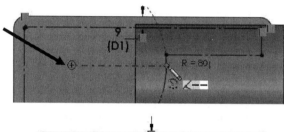

Sometimes when you convert sketch geometry, unwanted arcs and points are created. In the next section, delete any unwanted sketch geometry to cleanly create Sketch12.

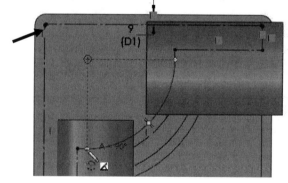

21. **Remove** the top left fillet with the Trim Entities Sketch tool.

22. **Restore** the corner of the fillet feature with the Trim Entities Sketch tool (Corner option) or by just dragging the endpoints together.

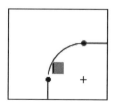 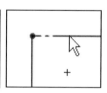

23. **Remove** all unwanted sketch geometry around the end point of the 90⁰ Arc.

Now you can utilize the horizontal and vertical construction geometry with the 9mm offset with new lines and the Arc is created correctly. Again there are other ways to create the sketch for the Extruded Cut feature.

24. **Complete** the close sketch profile with the Line Sketch tool.

Insert all needed Geometric relations.

25. **Insert** a vertical relation between the end point of the Arc and the corner point of the Thin-Extrude1 feature. The sketch should be fully defined and displayed in black.

26. **Create** the Extruded Cut feature. Apply the Up To Surface End Condition and click the inside face of Cut-Extrude3. The two surfaces provide a similar dimension.

27. **Apply** the Fillet feature. Insert three fillets per the provided drawing. 10mm is the fillet radius.

At this time your model should have a mass of **12154.09 grams**.

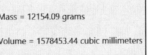

Mass = 12154.09 grams

Volume = 1578453.44 cubic millimeters

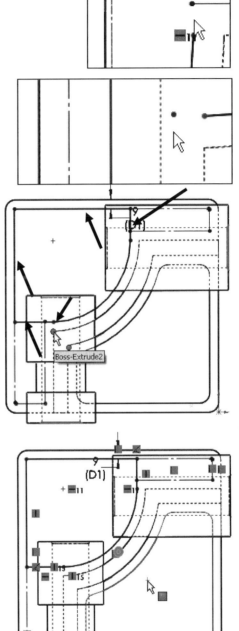

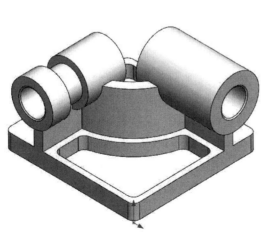

28. **Display** the Equations, Global Variables and Dimension dialog box.

29. **Enter** the five new Global Variables (A, B, C, D, & E) and the new Y equation as illustrated.

A = 221 mm
B = 211 mm
C = 165 mm
D = 121 mm
E = 37 mm
X = A/3
Y = B/3 + 15mm

Note: The equation for Y has changed from the initial part.

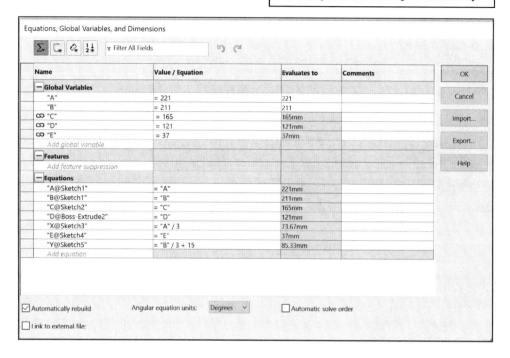

30. **Calculate** the mass of the model.

31. **Select 13206.40** grams.

32. **Save** the part.

33. **Rename** Part4 to Part5.

Always save your models to verify your results.

Use the Comments box to label your equations.

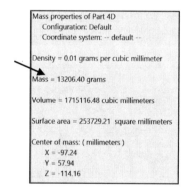

Mass properties of Part 4D
  Configuration: Default
  Coordinate system: -- default --

Density = 0.01 grams per cubic millimeter

Mass = 13206.40 grams

Volume = 1715116.48 cubic millimeters

Surface area = 253729.21 square millimeters

Center of mass: (millimeters)
  X = -97.24
  Y = 57.94
  Z = -114.16

Confirm that your math is correct. Use the Measure tool during the exam.

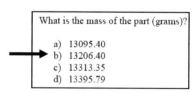

What is the mass of the part (grams)?

  a) 13095.40
  b) 13206.40
  c) 13313.35
  d) 13395.79

Segment 1 of the CSWP CORE exam - Fifth question

Compare the provided information with your existing part. The Global Variables
A thru E change and the equations are the same from the last question but
equation Y has changed from the initial part. This question provides a fill in the blank
format.

Provided Information:

5. Stage 2 - Update Parameters

Unit system: MMGS (millimeter, gram, second)

Decimal places: 2

Part origin: Arbitrary

Material: Alloy Steel

Density: 0.0077 g/mm^3

All holes through all unless shown otherwise.

Use the following parameters and equations which correspond to the dimensions labeled
in the images:

A = 229 mm

B = 217 mm

C = 163 mm

D = 119 mm

E = 34 mm

X = A/3

Y = B/3 + 15mm

Hint #1: The dimensions that are to be linked or updated and are variable will be labeled
with letters. Any dimensions that are simple value changes from one stage to another will
be circled in the images.

Hint #2: To save the most time, make use of linked dimensional values and equations.

Measure the mass of the part.

What is the mass of the part (grams)?

Let's begin.

1. **Display** the Equations, Global Variables and Dimensions dialog box.

2. **Enter** the five new Global Variables (A, B, C, D, & E) as illustrated.

A = 229 mm	
B = 217 mm	
C = 163 mm	
D = 119 mm	
E = 34 mm	
X = A/3	
Y = B/3 + 15mm	

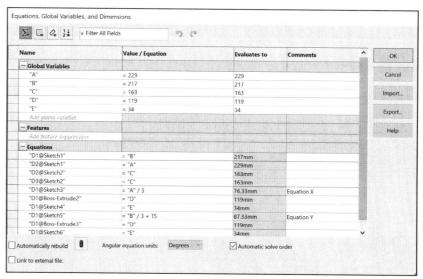

3. **Calculate** the mass of the part.

4. **Enter 14208.01** grams.

5. **Save** the part.

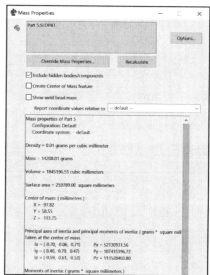

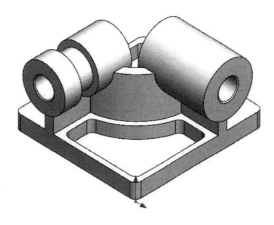

Segment 1 of the CSWP CORE exam - Additional Practice Problems

In this section, there are fewer step-by-step procedures. Use the provided initial and final models with the rollback bar if needed.

Question 1:
Build the following part in SOLIDWORKS.

Provided information:

Units: MMGS (millimeter, gram, second)

Decimal Places: 2

Part Origin: Arbitrary

Material: 6061 Alloy

Density: 2700 kg/m^2

All holes through all unless shown otherwise.

Use the following parameters and equations which correspond to the dimensions labeled in the images:

A: 60 mm

B: 45 mm

C: 52 degrees

D: 20 mm

X: 175 + D/2

What is the mass of the part in (grams)?

a) 686.50

b) 1858.61

c) 1845.10

d) 1742.88

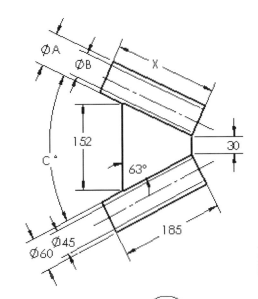

There are numerous ways to build the model in this section. A goal is to display different design intents and techniques.

Let's begin.

Create a new part in SOLIDWORKS.

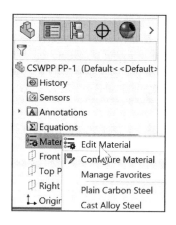

1. **Create** a folder to save your models.

2. **Create** a new part. Name it CSWPP PP-1.

3. **Set** document properties (drafting standard, units, and precision) for the model.

4. **Assign** 6061 Alloy material.

Address Global Variables and Equations.

5. **Display** the Equations, Global Variables, and Dimensions dialog box is displayed.

6. **Enter** the below information for the provided parameters and equations as illustrated.

7. **Click** OK from the dialog box.

8. **Expand** the Equations folder in the FeatureManager.

9. **View** the results.

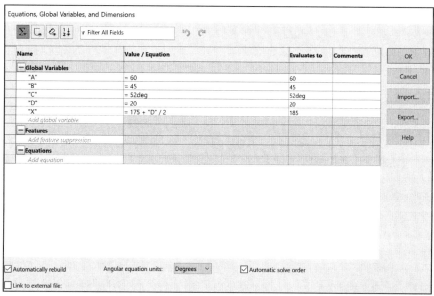

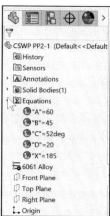

Start the Base feature (Boss-Extrude1) with Sketch1.

10. **Create** Sketch1. Select the Front plane and utilize Global Variable C.

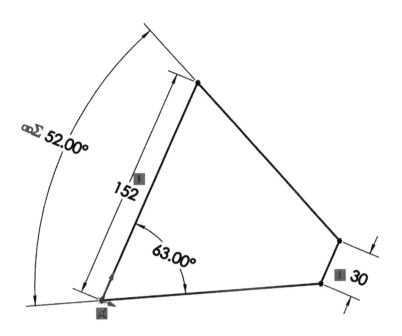

11. **Create** Boss-Extrude1. Apply the Mid-Plane End Condition with a distance of 20mm. Link the extruded distance to the Global Variable D. Currently your mass is **614.36 grams**.

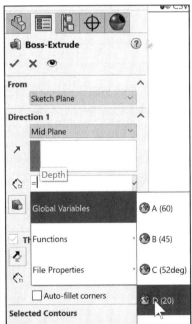

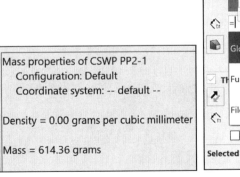

Mass properties of CSWP PP2-1
   Configuration: Default
   Coordinate system: -- default --

Density = 0.00 grams per cubic millimeter

Mass = 614.36 grams

12. **Create** Sketch2 on the Front plane for the Revolve1 feature. Use the Convert Entities and Offset Entities sketch tool. Address needed sketch relations and dimensions. Zoom in to select the correct references.

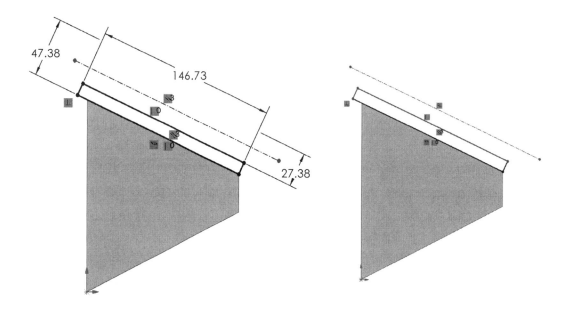

13. **Utilize** Global Variables. Note: There are many different ways to create this model.

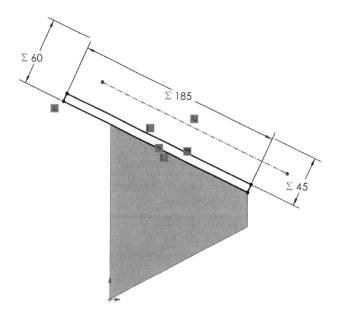

The CSWP exam in this section provides variables that either increase or decrease from the original part question. Design for this during the exam.

14. **Create** Revolve1 about the centerline. Revolve1 is the top tube feature. At this time your model should have a mass of **1232.24 grams**.

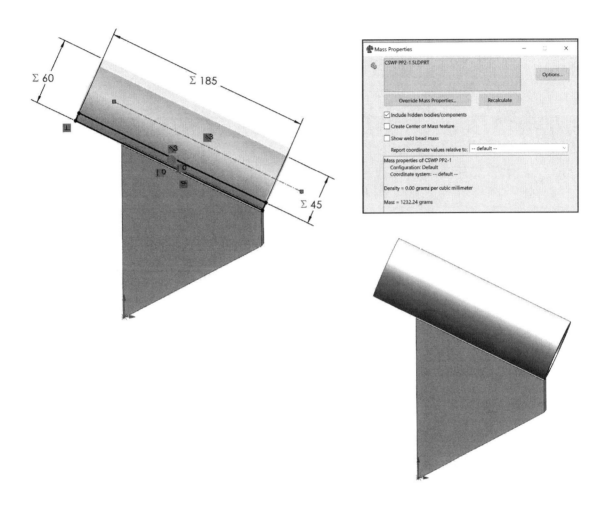

Merge the two bodies.

15. **Create** Sketch3. Select the top face of Boss-Extrude1. Utilize the Convert entities Sketch tool.

16. **Create** Boss-Extrude2. Extrude Up to Next (End Condition) making a single (Merge results) body part. At this time your model should have a mass of 1236.45 grams.

17. **Save** the part.

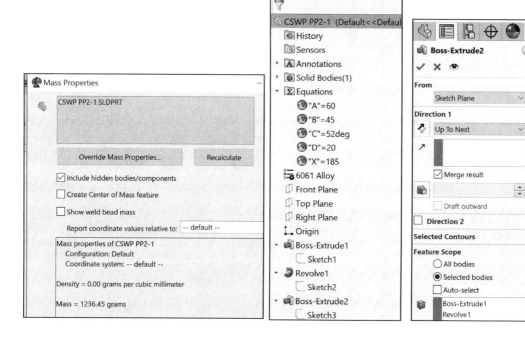

Create the bottom tube with a second Revolve feature.

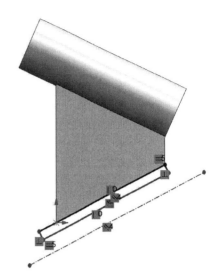

18. **Create** Sketch4 on the Front plane for the Revolve2 feature. You can use the Convert Entities and Offset Entities sketch tool. Address all needed sketch relations. Zoom in to select the correct references.

19. **Utilize** Global Variables. Note: There are many different ways to create this model.

20. **Create** Revolve2 about the centerline. Revolve2 is the bottom tube feature as illustrated. At this time your model should have a mass of **1854.33 grams**.

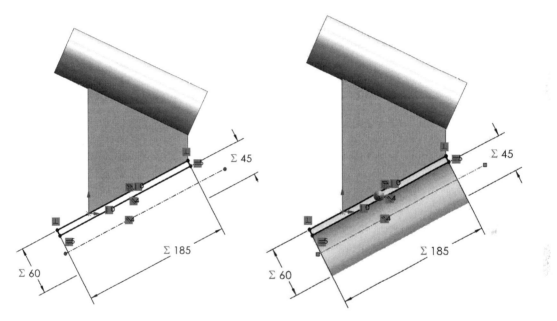

Mass properties of CSWP PP2-1
    Configuration: Default
    Coordinate system: -- default --

Density = 0.00 grams per cubic millimeter

Mass = 1854.33 grams

Volume = 686789.04 cubic millimeters

Surface area = 153882.29 square millimeters

Merge the two bodies.

21. **Create** Sketch5. Select the bottom face of Boss-Extrude1. Utilize the Convert Entities Sketch tool.

22. **Create** Boss-Extrude3. Extrude Up to Next (End Condition) making a single (Merge results) body part.

23. **Calculate** the mass of the model in grams.

24. **Enter 1858.61** grams. In the CSWP exam you will need to enter this number exactly. You need to be within 0.5% of the stated value in the single answer format to get this question correct.

25. **Save** the part.

26. **Rename** the CSWP PP2-1 part to CSWP PP2-2.

What is the mass of the part in (grams)?
a) 1686.50

b) 1858.61

c) 1845.10

d) 1742.88

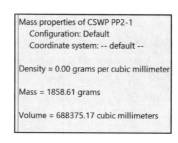 This section presents a representation of the types of questions that you will see in this segment of the exam.

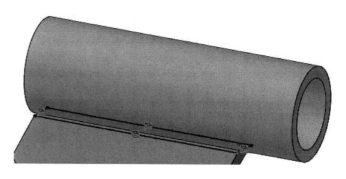

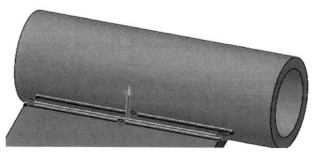

Mass properties of CSWP PP2-1
Configuration: Default
Coordinate system: -- default --

Density = 0.00 grams per cubic millimeter

Mass = 1858.61 grams

Volume = 688375.17 cubic millimeters

Question 1: Part II

Compare the provided information with the existing part (CSWP PP2-2) which you created in the previous section. Use the provided initial and final models with the rollback bar if needed.

What is the mass of the part in grams?

Provided information:

Units: MMGS (millimeter, gram, second)

Decimal Places: 2

Part Origin: Arbitrary

Material: 6061 Alloy

Density: 2700 kg/m^2

All holes through all unless shown otherwise.

Use the following parameters and equations which correspond to the dimensions labeled in the images.

A: 80 mm

B: 60 mm

C: 50 degree

D: 40 mm

X: 180 + D/2

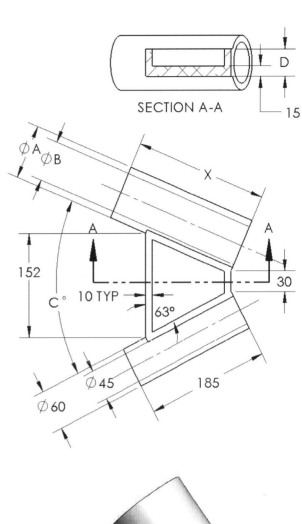

SECTION A-A

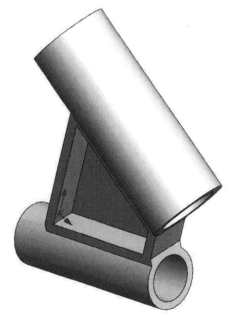

Let's begin.

Compare the provided **dimensions, materials, variables** and **equation**.

Question 1:
Build the following part in SOLIDWORKS.

Provided information:

Units: MMGS (millimeter, gram, second)

Decimal Places: 2

Part Origin: Arbitrary

Material: 6061 Alloy

Density: 2700 kg/m²

All holes through all unless shown otherwise.

Use the following parameters and equations which correspond to the dimensions labeled in the images:

A: 60 mm

B: 45 mm

C: 52 degrees

D: 20 mm

X: 175 + D/2

What is the mass of the part in (grams)?

a) 686.50

b) 1858.61

c) 1845.10

d) 1742.88

Question 1: Part II

Compare the provided information with the existing part (CSWP PP2-2) which you created in the previous section. Use the provided initial and final models with the rollback bar if needed.

What is the mass of the part in grams?

Provided information:

Units: MMGS (millimeter, gram, second)

Decimal Places: 2

Part Origin: Arbitrary

Material: 6061 Alloy

Density: 2700 kg/m²

All holes through all unless shown otherwise.

Use the following parameters and equations which correspond to the dimensions labeled in the images.

A: 80 mm

B: 60 mm

C: 50 degree

D: 40 mm

X: 180 + D/2

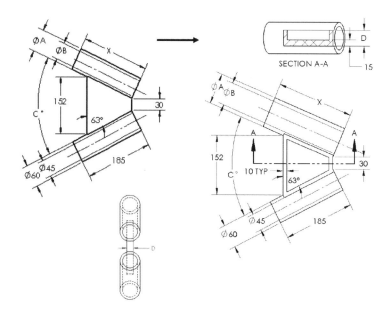

Where do you start? Three variables and the equation were changed. Edit the Equations, Global Variables, and Dimensions dialog box.

A: 60 mm	**A**: 80 mm
B: 45 mm	**B**: 60 mm
C: 52 degrees	**C**: 50 degree
D: 20 mm	**D**: 40 mm
X: 175 + D/2	**X**: 180 + D/2

1. **Right-click** the Equations folder. Click Manager Equations. The Equations, Global Variables, and Dimensions dialog box is displayed.

Equations, Global Variables, and Dimensions

Σ | ⊑ | ✎ | 1↓2↓ | ▾ Filter All Fields | ↶ ↷

Name	Value / Equation	Evaluates to	Comments	
Global Variables				OK
∞ "A"	= 80	80mm		Cancel
∞ "B"	= 60	60mm		
∞ "C"	= 50deg	50deg		Import...
"D"	= 40	40		Export...
∞ "X"	= 180 + "D" / 2	200mm		
Add global variable				Help
Features				
Add feature suppression				
Equations				
"D1@Boss-Extrude1"	= "D"	40mm		
Add equation				

2. **Enter** the above information for the provided parameters and equation as illustrated.

3. **Click** OK from the dialog box.

At this time your model should have a mass of **3153.76 grams**.

4. **Expand** the Equations folder. View the results.

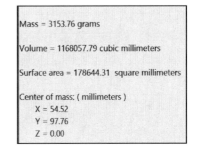

Mass = 3153.76 grams

Volume = 1168057.79 cubic millimeters

Surface area = 178644.31 square millimeters

Center of mass: (millimeters)
  X = 54.52
  Y = 97.76
  Z = 0.00

Address the Offset Extruded Cut feature displayed in the illustration.

5. **Create** Sketch6 on the front face of the plate. Utilize the Offset Entities Sketch tool. Enter 10mm depth to the inside.

6. **Display** an Isometric view to create the Extruded Cut feature.

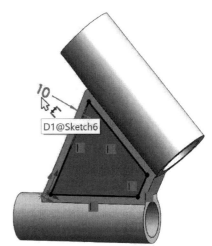

D1@Sketch6

7. **Create** Cut-Extrude1. Utilize the Offset from Surface End Condition. Select the back face. Enter 15mm (Depth) as illustrated.

8. **Save** the part.

9. **Calculate** the mass of the model in grams.

What is the mass of the part in grams?

10. **Enter 2531.70** grams.

11. **Rename** part CSWP PP2-2 to CSWP PP2-3.

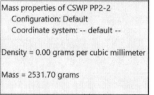

Mass properties of CSWP PP2-2
    Configuration: Default
    Coordinate system: -- default --

Density = 0.00 grams per cubic millimeter

Mass = 2531.70 grams

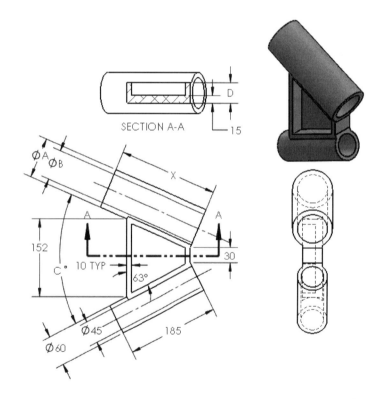

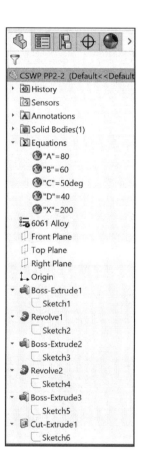

Question 1: Part III

Build the following part in SOLIDWORKS.

Compare the provided information (dimensions, material, variables and equation) with the existing part (CSWP PP2-3) which you created in the previous section.

What is the mass of the part in grams?

Provided Information:

Units: MMGS (millimeter, gram, second)

Decimal Places: 2

Part Origin: Arbitrary

Material: 6061 Alloy

Density: 2700 kg/m^2

All holes through all unless shown otherwise.

Use the following parameters and equations which correspond to the dimensions labeled in the images.

A: 80 mm

B: 60 mm

C: 50 degrees

D: 40 mm

X: 180 + D/2

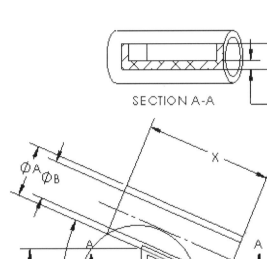

SECTION A-A

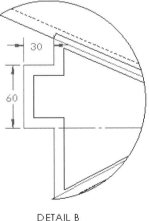

DETAIL B

Let's begin.

Compare the **dimensions**, **material**, **variables** and **equation**.

Question 1: Part II

Compare the provided information with the existing part (CSWP PP2-2) which you created in the previous section. Use the provided initial and final models with the rollback bar if needed.

What is the mass of the part in grams?

Provided information:

Units: MMGS (millimeter, gram, second)

Decimal Places: 2

Part Origin: Arbitrary

Material: 6061 Alloy

Density: 2700 kg/m²

All holes through all unless shown otherwise.

Use the following parameters and equations which correspond to the dimensions labeled in the images.

A: 80 mm

B: 60 mm

C: 50 degree

D: 40 mm

X: 180 + D/2

→

Question 1: Part III

Build the following part in SOLIDWORKS.

Compare the provided information (dimensions, material, variables and equation) with the existing part (CSWP PP2-3) which you created in the previous section.

What is the mass of the part in grams?

Provided Information:

Units: MMGS (millimeter, gram, second)

Decimal Places: 2

Part Origin: Arbitrary

Material: 6061 Alloy

Density: 2700 kg/m²

All holes through all unless shown otherwise.

Use the following parameters and equations which correspond to the dimensions labeled in the images.

A: 80 mm

B: 60 mm

C: 50 degrees

D: 40 mm

X: 180 + D/2

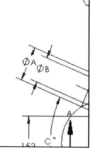

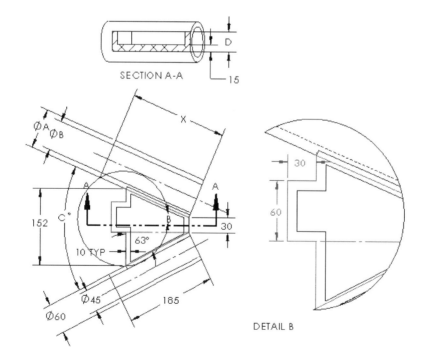

SECTION A-A

DETAIL B

None of the variables or equation was modified between the second and third question. Start with the first Boss-Extrude1 feature.

1. **Drag** the rollback bar directly under Boss-Extrude1.

2. **Edit** the base sketch (Sketch1) according to the Detail view. Create a 30mm x 60mm corner rectangle. Trim geometry.

A: 80 mm	A: 80 mm
B: 60 mm	B: 60 mm
C: 50 degree	C: 50 degree
D: 40 mm	D: 40 mm
X: 180 + D/2	X: 180 + D/2

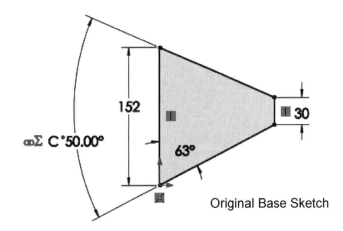

Original Base Sketch

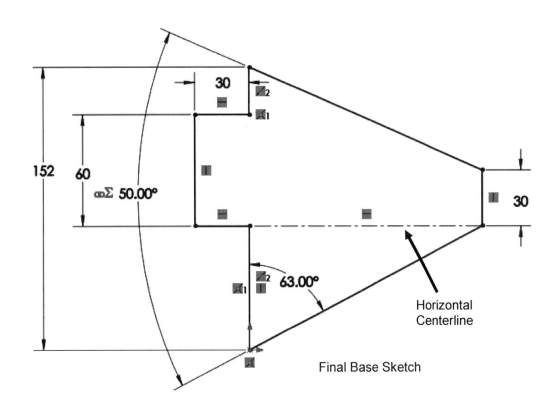

Final Base Sketch

3. **Save** the part.

4. **Calculate** the mass of the model in grams.

What is the mass of the part in grams?

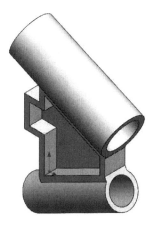

5. **Enter 2645.10** grams.

Always enter the needed decimal places in the answer field.

Mass properties of CSWP PP2-3
  Configuration: Default
  Coordinate system: -- default --

Density = 0.00 grams per cubic millimeter

Mass = 2645.10 grams

You are finished with this section. Good luck on the Segment 1 exam.

During the exam, utilize the various drawing view options and zoom tool to better understand the location of fillets and rounds. Fillets and rounds are displayed in red.

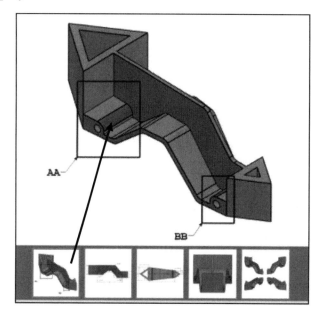

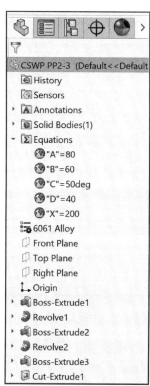

Below are former screen shots from a previous CSWP exam in Segment 1.

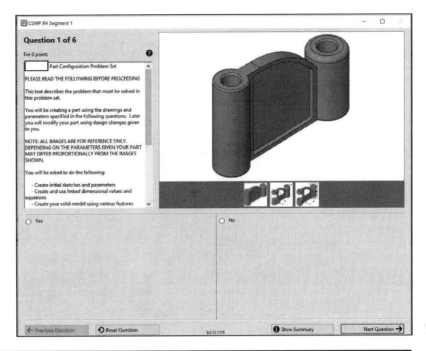

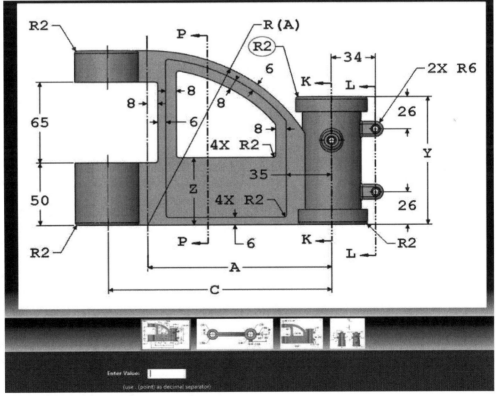

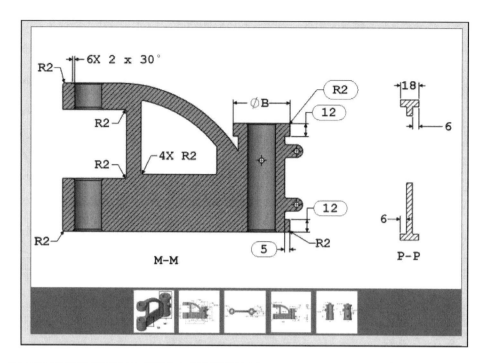

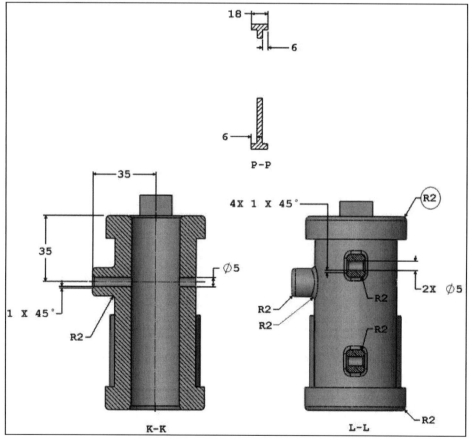

The changes between parts in each question are concentrated in indicated areas as shown below with a box or circle.

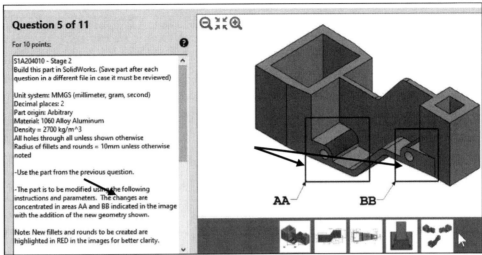

Question 5 of 11

For 10 points:

S1A204010 - Stage 2
Build this part in SolidWorks. (Save part after each question in a different file in case it must be reviewed)

Unit system: MMGS (millimeter, gram, second)
Decimal places: 2
Part origin: Arbitrary
Material: 1060 Alloy Aluminum
Density = 2700 kg/m^3
All holes through all unless shown otherwise
Radius of fillets and rounds = 10mm unless otherwise noted

-Use the part from the previous question.

-The part is to be modified using the following instructions and parameters. The changes are concentrated in areas AA and BB indicated in the image with the addition of the new geometry shown.

Note: New fillets and rounds to be created are highlighted in RED in the images for better clarity.

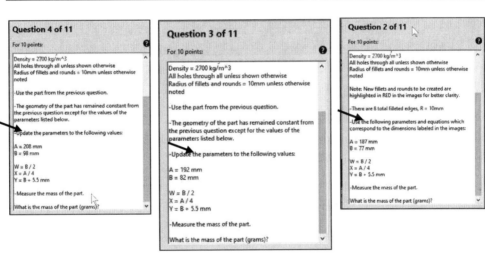

Question 4 of 11

For 10 points:

Density = 2700 kg/m^3
All holes through all unless shown otherwise
Radius of fillets and rounds = 10mm unless otherwise noted

-Use the part from the previous question.

-The geometry of the part has remained constant from the previous question except for the values of the parameters listed below.

-Update the parameters to the following values:

A = 208 mm
B = 98 mm

W = B / 2
X = A / 4
Y = B + 5.5 mm

-Measure the mass of the part.

What is the mass of the part (grams)?

Question 3 of 11

For 10 points:

Density = 2700 kg/m^3
All holes through all unless shown otherwise
Radius of fillets and rounds = 10mm unless otherwise noted

-Use the part from the previous question.

-The geometry of the part has remained constant from the previous question except for the values of the parameters listed below.

-Update the parameters to the following values:

A = 192 mm
B = 82 mm

W = B / 2
X = A / 4
Y = B + 5.5 mm

-Measure the mass of the part.

What is the mass of the part (grams)?

Question 2 of 11

For 10 points:

Density = 2700 kg/m^3
All holes through all unless shown otherwise
Radius of fillets and rounds = 10mm unless otherwise noted

Note: New fillets and rounds to be created are highlighted in RED in the images for better clarity.

-There are 8 total filleted edges, R = 10mm

-Use the following parameters and equations which correspond to the dimensions labeled in the images:

A = 187 mm
B = 77 mm

W = B / 2
X = A / 4
Y = B + 5.5 mm

-Measure the mass of the part.

What is the mass of the part (grams)?

Notes:

CHAPTER 2 - SEGMENT 2 OF THE CORE CSWP EXAM

Introduction

Segment 2 of the CSWP exam is 50 minutes long with twelve (12) questions divided into three categories. The segment focuses on part modifications and configurations.

The format is either multiple-choice or single fill in the blank.

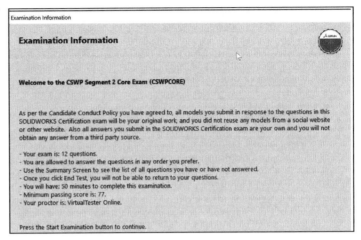

The first question is an instructional page. Read the instructions. Agree to the Candidate Conduct Policy. Click Yes. It's a free 5 points.

Click the link to download the needed part files.

Save the downloaded part files to a working folder, (Extract All). Note: You should have 3 parts.

Segment 2 requires knowledge of the following:

- Download and open a zip file

- Open a part

- Apply material

- Modify part geometry

- Use the Meassure and Mass Properties tool

- Apply sketch tools and sketch relations

- Recognize Engineering drawing views with annotations

- Recover from rebuild errors

- Understand configurations

- Analyze configurations

- Create new configurations

- Modify existing configurations

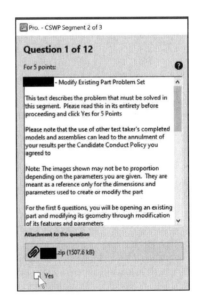

Question 2: Open the required part. The second question is in a multiple-choice format. Read the question. Select an answer. Click Next Question. All answers are in the MMGS unit standard. Decimal place 2.

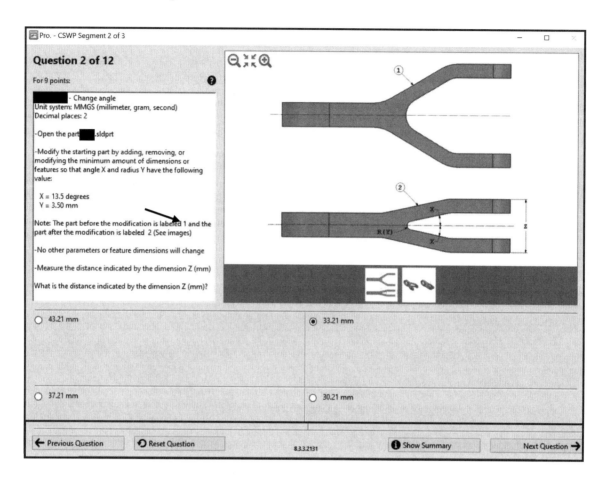

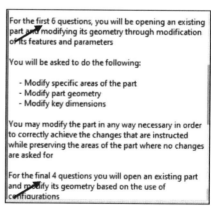

The first 6 questions, you will be opening two existing parts and modifying their geometry through modification of their features and parameters.

For the final 4 questions you will open an existing part and modify its geometry based on the use of configurations.

If you don't have the exact answer, (within 0.5% of the stated value in the multiple-choice section) you will most likely fail the following questions (3, 4 and 5).

Note: The part before the modification is labeled 1, and the part after the modification is labeled 2. View the provided images in the exam.

Questions 3, 4, and 5 are in a single answer format. Question 3: Modify the part from the last question (question 2). Enter the answer. Decimal place 2. Click Next Question.

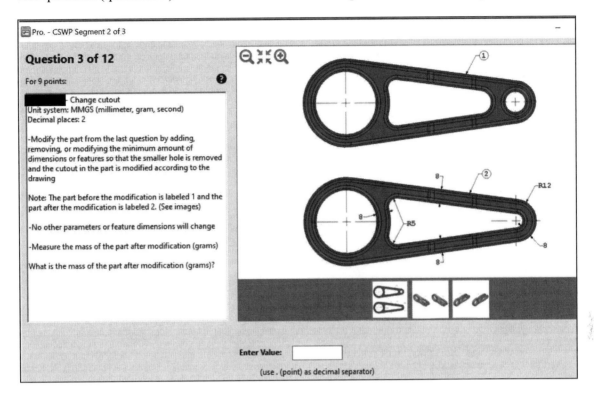

Question 4: Modify the part from the last question (question 3). Single answer format. Remove pocket from one side of the part. Enter the answer. Decimal place 2. Click Next Question.

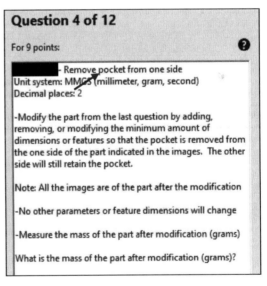

Question 5: Modify the part from the last question (question 4). Remove all fillets and inner pocket. Modify wall thickness. View all images which are provided. Enter the answer. Decimal place 2. Click Next Question.

Question 6: Open a new part. Multiple-choice format. Read the question. Select an answer. Click Next Question.

You should have the exact answer (within 0.5% of the stated value in the multiple-choice section) before you move on to the next question.

If you don't have the exact answer, you will most likely fail the following question. This is crucial as there is no partial credit.

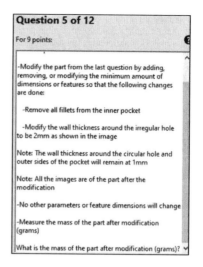

Question 5 of 12

For 9 points:

-Modify the part from the last question by adding, removing, or modifying the minimum amount of dimensions or features so that the following changes are done:

-Remove all fillets from the inner pocket

-Modify the wall thickness around the irregular hole to be 2mm as shown in the image

Note: The wall thickness around the circular hole and outer sides of the pocket will remain at 1mm

Note: All the images are of the part after the modification

-No other parameters or feature dimensions will change

-Measure the mass of the part after modification (grams)

What is the mass of the part after modification (grams)?

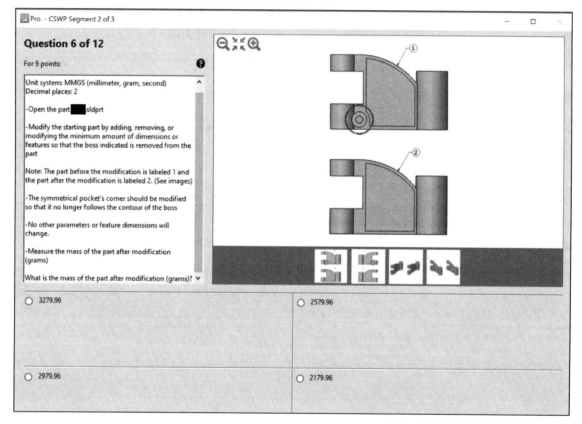

Pro. - CSWP Segment 2 of 3

Question 6 of 12

For 9 points:

Unit system: MMGS (millimeter, gram, second)
Decimal places: 2

-Open the part ▮ sldprt

-Modify the starting part by adding, removing, or modifying the minimum amount of dimensions or features so that the boss indicated is removed from the part

Note: The part before the modification is labeled 1 and the part after the modification is labeled 2. (See images)

-The symmetrical pocket's corner should be modified so that it no longer follows the contour of the boss

-No other parameters or feature dimensions will change.

-Measure the mass of the part after modification (grams)

What is the mass of the part after modification (grams)?

○ 3279.96   ○ 2579.96

○ 2979.96   ○ 2179.96

Note: The part before the modification is labeled 1, and the part after the modification is labeled 2. View the provided images in the exam.

Question 7: Add grooves. Single answer format. Enter the answer. Decimal place 2. Click Next Question.

Question 8: Open a new part. Multiple-choice format. Read the question. Select an answer. Click Next Question.

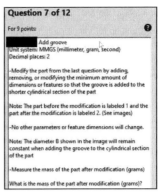

Question 7 of 12

For 9 points:

Add groove
Unit system: MMGS (millimeter, gram, second)
Decimal places: 2

-Modify the part from the last question by adding, removing, or modifying the minimum amount of dimensions or features so that the groove is added to the shorter cylindrical section of the part

Note: The part before the modification is labeled 1 and the part after the modification is labeled 2. (See images)

-No other parameters or feature dimensions will change.

Note: The diameter B shown in the image will remain constant when adding the groove to the cylindrical section of the part

-Measure the mass of the part after modification (grams)

What is the mass of the part after modification (grams)?

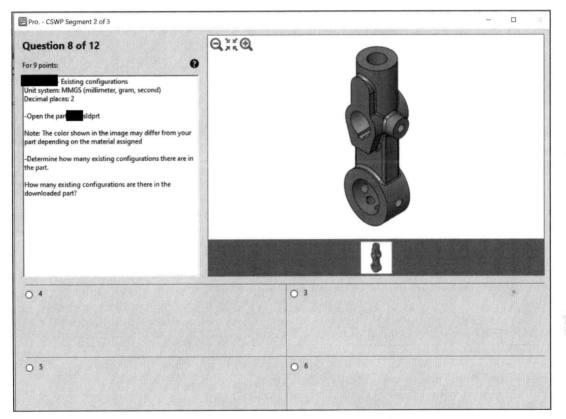

Pro. - CSWP Segment 2 of 3

Question 8 of 12

For 9 points:

_____: Existing configurations
Unit system: MMGS (millimeter, gram, second)
Decimal places: 2

-Open the par____.sldprt

Note: The color shown in the image may differ from your part depending on the material assigned

-Determine how many existing configurations there are in the part.

How many existing configurations are there in the downloaded part?

○ 4   ○ 3

○ 5   ○ 6

Question 9: Using the part from the last question (question 8), switch to Configuration C. Single answer format. Enter the answer. Decimal place 2. Click Next Question.

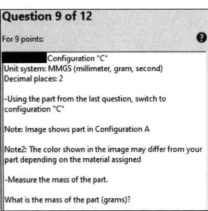

Question 9 of 12

For 9 points:

_____Configuration "C"
Unit system: MMGS (millimeter, gram, second)
Decimal places: 2

-Using the part from the last question, switch to configuration "C"

Note: Image shows part in Configuration A

Note2: The color shown in the image may differ from your part depending on the material assigned

-Measure the mass of the part.

What is the mass of the part (grams)?

Question 10: Multiple-choice format. Read the question. Select an answer. Click Next Question.

Note: The question states, "Copy and Paste to create a new configuration Z may (it will) lead to an error in feature E9 in the new configuration. If you decide to use the Copy and Paste method, repair this error in the feature E9 before you continue."

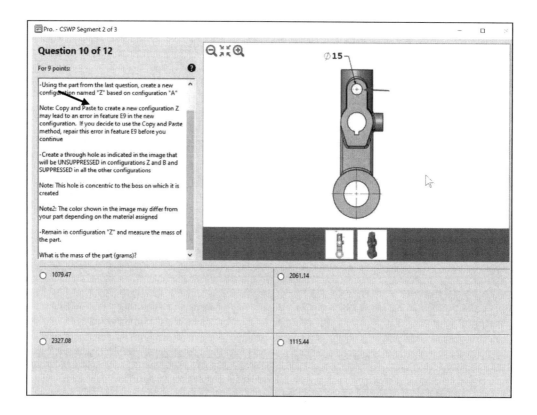

You will see an error! Click Stop and Repair from the SOLIDWORKS dialog box.

Click Close from the What's Wrong dialog box.

Normally, E9 is an Extruded Cut feature looking for a face or surface.

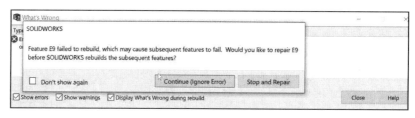

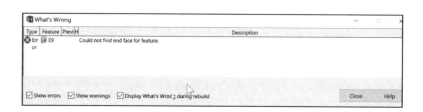

Question 11: Read the question. Single answer format. Enter the answer. Decimal place 2. Click Next Question.

Question 12: Multiple-choice format. Read the question. Select the answers. Click Next Question. This is the last question in the exam.

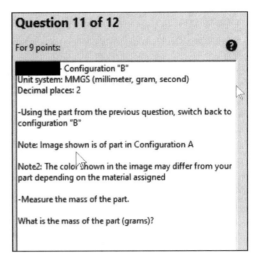

Question 11 of 12

For 9 points: ❓

███████ - Configuration "B"
Unit system: MMGS (millimeter, gram, second)
Decimal places: 2

-Using the part from the previous question, switch back to configuration "B"

Note: Image shown is of part in Configuration A

Note2: The color shown in the image may differ from your part depending on the material assigned

-Measure the mass of the part.

What is the mass of the part (grams)?

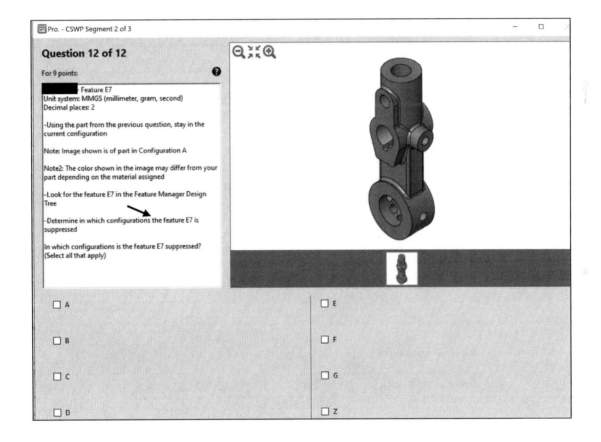

Pro. - CSWP Segment 2 of 3

Question 12 of 12

For 9 points: ❓

███████ - Feature E7
Unit system: MMGS (millimeter, gram, second)
Decimal places: 2

-Using the part from the previous question, stay in the current configuration

Note: Image shown is of part in Configuration A

Note2: The color shown in the image may differ from your part depending on the material assigned

-Look for the feature E7 in the Feature Manager Design Tree

-Determine in which configurations the feature E7 is suppressed

In which configurations is the feature E7 suppressed? (Select all that apply)

☐ A   ☐ E

☐ B   ☐ F

☐ C   ☐ G

☐ D   ☐ Z

A total score of 77 out of 104 or better is required to pass.

If you fail this segment of the exam, you need to wait 14 days before you can retake it. In that time, you can take another segment.

The images displayed on the exam are not to scale due to differences in the parts being downloaded for each tester.

Utilize the provided segment model folders to follow along while using the book.

Download all needed model files (initial and final) and the SOLIDWORKS CSWP Sample Exam folder from the SDC Publications website (www.SDCpublications.com/downloads/978-1-63057-542-7).

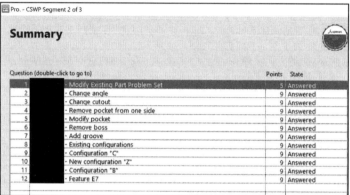

If your school is an academic certification provider, your instructor can allocate a free exam credit for the CSWP (Segment 1, Segment 2 or Segment 3). The instructor will require your .edu email address.

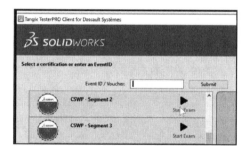

Segment 2 of the CSWP CORE Exam

Create a folder to save your working models. The first question is an instructional page. Read the instructions. Click Yes. Click the link to download the needed files

Save the downloaded files to a working folder, (Extract All).

Open the Sample6 part from the provided Segment 2 Initial folder. This is one of the downloaded parts for this segment.

Let's begin.

Open the SOLIDWORKS part. A question in this section could be - determine how many existing configurations there are in the part.

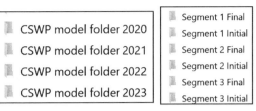

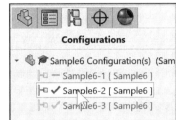

1. **Create** a folder to save your working model.

2. **Open** the Sample6 part from the Segment 2 Initial folder.

3. **Click** the ConfigurationManager tab in the design tree.

4. **View** the different configurations of the part.

5. **Select 3** for the number of configurations in the multiple-choice answer section of the exam.

6. **Double-click** on each configuration in the ConfigurationManager. The FeatureManager displays a different material for each configuration.

It is important that you understand that these materials will change in the exam, and to understand where you would start a new configuration to the existing ConfigurationManager.

A question in this section could be - create a new configuration (Sample6-4) from the existing Sample6-3 configuration.

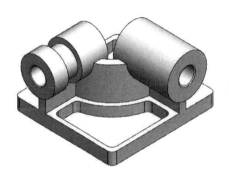

Calculate the mass of the new configuration (Sample6-4) in grams. **Decimal places**: 2.

Let's begin.

7. **Double-click** Sample6-3. Sample6-3 is the active Configuration.

8. **Add** a new configuration Sample6-4. Sample6-4 is the current configuration. Note: You can also use the Copy/Paste command.

9. **Calculate** the mass of the new configuration Sample6-4 in grams.

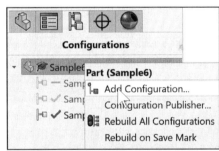

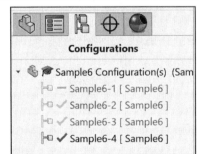

10. **Enter 4982.03** grams for the answer. It is important to input the proper decimal places as requested in the exam.

11. **Save** the model.

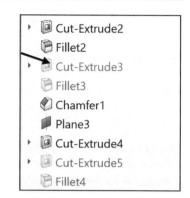

Configuration: Sample6-4
Coordinate system: -- default --

Density = 0.00 grams per cubic millimeter

Mass = 4982.03 grams

A question in this section could be - suppress a feature in some but not all configurations.

Suppress the front cut (Cut-Extrude3) and back cut (Cut-Extrude5) in the Sample6-4 configuration.

Note: The Cut-Extrude3 feature references the Fillet3, Cut-Extrude5, and Fillet4 feature in the provided model.

Calculate the mass of the part in grams. Decimal places: 2.

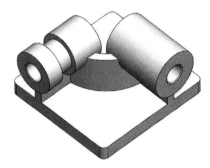

Let's begin.

There are numerous ways to address the models in this segment. A goal is to display different design intents and techniques.

12. **Suppress** the feature as illustrated in the Sample6-4 configuration.

13. **Calculate** the Mass Properties of configuration sample6-4 with the suppressed features.

14. **Enter 6423.17** grams for the answer. You need to be within 0.5% of the stated value in the single answer format to get this question correct.

15. **Save** the part.

A question in this section could be - create configuration Sample6-5 from configuration Sample6-1.

Provided Information:

Add a 30x30x10mm square in the *front left corner* of (Boss-Extrude1). Utilize the existing fillet radius as the Base Extrude1 feature in your sketch.

Calculate the mass of the part in grams.

Decimal places: 2.

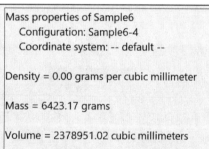

Mass properties of Sample6
   Configuration: Sample6-4
   Coordinate system: -- default --

Density = 0.00 grams per cubic millimeter

Mass = 6423.17 grams

Volume = 2378951.02 cubic millimeters

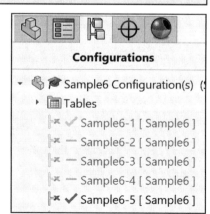

Configurations

Sample6 Configuration(s) (
  Tables
    Sample6-1 [Sample6]
    Sample6-2 [Sample6]
    Sample6-3 [Sample6]
    Sample6-4 [Sample6]
    Sample6-5 [Sample6]

Let's begin.

16. **Double-click** the Sample6-1 configuration from the ConfigurationManager. Sample6-1 is the active configuration.

17. **Add** a new configuration sample6-5. Sample6-5 is the current configuration.

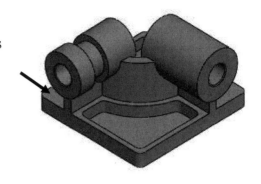

Create the sketch for the 30x30x10 mm square. Control the sketch with geometric relations and dimensions. Do not select the midpoint of the horizontal line segment.

☀ Utilize the split bar to work between the FeatureManager and the ConfigurationManager.

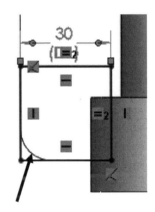

18. **Create** the sketch using the Corner Rectangle Sketch tool. Insert the needed geometric relation and dimension. Do not select the midpoint of the horizontal line segment.

Remember it stated, utilize the existing fillet radius as the Base Extrude1 feature in your sketch.

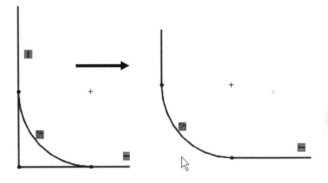

19. **Utilize** the Convert Entities Sketch tool along with the Trim Entitles Sketch tool to complete the sketch.

20. **Create** the Boss-Extrude feature with a depth of 10mm. Boss-Extrude4 is displayed in the FeatureManager.

21. **Calculate** the Mass Properties of configuration Sample6-5 with the new feature.

22. **Enter 16500.44** grams for the answer. It is very important to input the proper decimal places as requested in the exam.

23. **Save** the part.

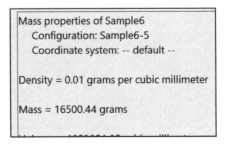

Mass properties of Sample6
    Configuration: Sample6-5
    Coordinate system: -- default --

Density = 0.01 grams per cubic millimeter

Mass = 16500.44 grams

A question in this section could be - create a new configuration Sample6-6 from configuration Sample6-2 in a design table by copying/pasting a new row.

Start with configuration Sample6-2.

Create a design table.

Create a new configuration Sample6-6 from configuration Sample6-2 in the design table by copying/pasting a new row.

Change the following parameter in the design table for configuration Sample6-6 to the following specified values:

- D1@Boss-Extrude1 = 35

Calculate the mass of the part in grams.

Decimal places: 2.

Let's begin.

1. **Double-click** Sample6-2. Sample6-2 is the active configuration.

2. **Create** an MS Excel design table. Use the Auto-create option.

3. **Create** a new configuration Sample6-6 (copy/paste) from Sample6-2 in the design table.

Design Table for: Sample6	$DESCRIPTION	$COLOR		$LIBRARY:MATERIAL@Sample6A	$STATE@Sketch13	$STATE@Boss-Extrude4	$STATE@Cut-Extrude3	$STATE@Fillet3	$STATE@Cut-Extrude5	$STATE@Fillet4
Sample 6-1	Sample 6-1	6191062	SOLIDWORKS Materials:Copper							
Sample6-2	Sample6-2	15266559	SOLIDWORKS Materials:Alloy Steel		S	S				
Sample6-3	Sample6-3	15266559	SOLIDWORKS Materials:6061 Alloy							
Sample6-4	Sample6-4	15266559	SOLIDWORKS Materials:6061 Alloy				S	S	S	S
Sample6-5	Sample6-5	6191062	SOLIDWORKS Materials:Copper							
Sample6-6	Sample6-2	15266559	SOLIDWORKS Materials:Alloy Steel		S	S				

Check your new configuration in the ConfigurationManager. Update the design table.

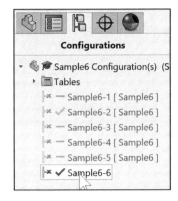

4. **Exit** the design table and view the new configuration Sample6-6 in the ConfigurationManager.

5. **Double-click** Sample6-6. Sample6-6 is the active configuration.

6. **Edit** the design table. Do not add any columns and rows to the table. View the updated design table.

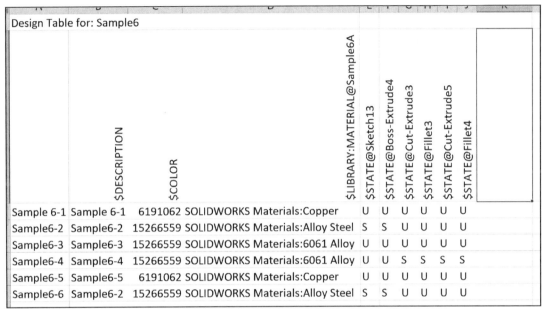

Design Table for: Sample6

	$DESCRIPTION	$COLOR	$LIBRARY:MATERIAL@Sample6A	$STATE@Sketch13	$STATE@Boss-Extrude4	$STATE@Cut-Extrude3	$STATE@Fillet3	$STATE@Cut-Extrude5	$STATE@Fillet4
Sample 6-1	Sample 6-1	6191062	SOLIDWORKS Materials:Copper	U	U	U	U	U	U
Sample6-2	Sample6-2	15266559	SOLIDWORKS Materials:Alloy Steel	S	S	U	U	U	U
Sample6-3	Sample6-3	15266559	SOLIDWORKS Materials:6061 Alloy	U	U	U	U	U	U
Sample6-4	Sample6-4	15266559	SOLIDWORKS Materials:6061 Alloy	U	U	S	S	S	S
Sample6-5	Sample6-5	6191062	SOLIDWORKS Materials:Copper	U	U	U	U	U	U
Sample6-6	Sample6-2	15266559	SOLIDWORKS Materials:Alloy Steel	S	S	U	U	U	U

Change the D1@Boss-Extrude1 = 35 parameter in the design table for configuration sample6-6.

7. **Double-click** on the Boss-Extrude1 feature. The column for the state of Boss-Extrude1 is displayed in the design table.

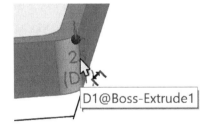

8. **Click** the depth dimension 25 in the Graphics window. 25 is displayed in the design table.

9. **Enter** 35, depth dimension for configuration Sample6-6.

10. **Exit** the design table.

11. **View** the new Sample6-6 configuration dimension.

$DESCRIPTION	$COLOR	$LIBRARY:MATERIAL@Sample6A	$STATE@Sketch13	$STATE@Boss-Extrude4	$STATE@Cut-Extrude3	$STATE@Fillet3	$STATE@Cut-Extrude5	$STATE@Fillet4	$STATE@Boss-Extrude1	D1@Boss-Extrude1
Sample 6-1	6191062	SOLIDWORKS Materials:Copper	U	U	U	U	U	U	UNSUPPRESSED	25
Sample6-2	15266559	SOLIDWORKS Materials:Alloy Steel	S	S	U	U	U	U		
Sample6-3	15266559	SOLIDWORKS Materials:6061 Alloy	U	U	U	U	U	U		
Sample6-4	15266559	SOLIDWORKS Materials:6061 Alloy	U	U	S	S	S	S		
Sample6-5	6191062	SOLIDWORKS Materials:Copper	U	U	U	U	U	U		
Sample6-6	15266559	SOLIDWORKS Materials:Alloy Steel	S	S	U	U	U	U		35

12. **Apply** the Measure tool to confirm the design table modification.

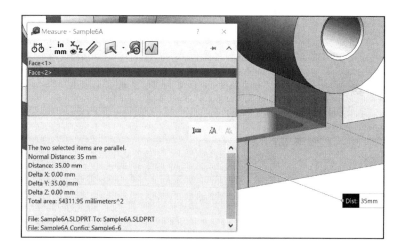

13. **Exit** the design table.

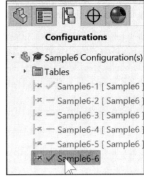

14. **Double-click** Sample6-6. Sample6-6 is the active configuration.

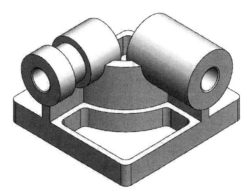

15. **Calculate** the Mass Properties of configuration Sample6-6. All answers are in the MMGS unit standard. Decimal place 2.

16. **Enter 16604.47** for the anwser. You are finished with the first category in Segment 2 of the CSWP CORE exam.

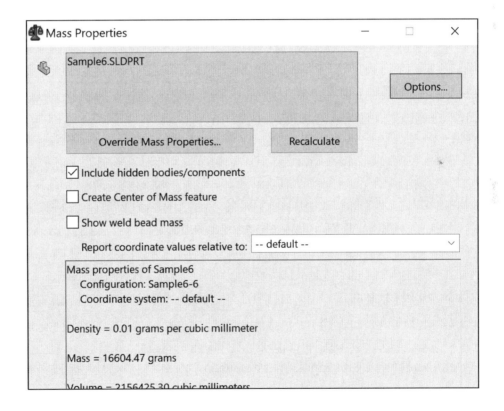

Second Category:

- Modify a part and recover from errors in this category. Edges, fillets and faces will be lost, and modify planes and sketches.

- Recover from rebuild errors while maintaining the overall design intent

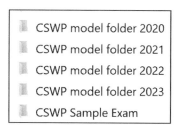

Let's begin.

A question in this section could be - determine the mass of the part in grams.

Decimal places: 2.

1. **Open** the Sample7-1 part from the Segment 2 Initial folder.

2. **Calculate** the mass of the part in grams. All answers are in the MMGS unit standard. Decimal place 2.

3. **Select 1443.72** grams in the multiple-choice answer section of the exam. The first question in this segment is typically in a multiple-choice format.

4. **Save** Sample7-1 as Sample7-2.

A question in this section could be - modify the large hole diameter from 25mm to 20mm.

Calculate the mass of the part in grams.

Let's begin.

First find the large hole and its initial value.

5. **Double-click** Cut-Extrude1. View the 25mm diameter.

6. **Enter** 20mm.

7. **Rebuild** the part.

8. **Calculate** the mass of the part in grams.

9. **Enter 1522.29** grams. Think about your answer. If you obtain a lower mass number when you have more material, something is wrong.

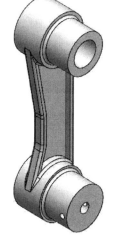

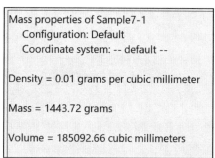

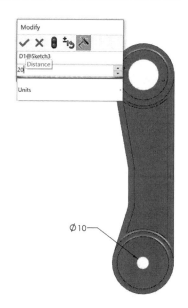

10. **Save** Sample7-2 as Sample7-3.

A question in this section could be - modify the shell thickness from 5mm to 4mm.

Calculate the mass of the part in grams.

Decimal places: 2.

Think about the effects of this modification on the mass of the part.

Let's begin.

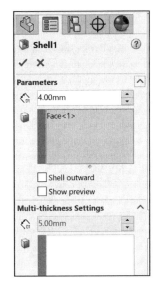

11. **Edit** Shell1 from the FeatureManager.

12. **Enter** 4mm for Thickness.

13. **Calculate** the mass of the part in grams.

14. **Enter 961.25** grams.

15. **Save** Sample7-3 as Sample7-4.

A question in this section could be - create a symmetrical handle between the two cylinders.

The handle is symmetrical both horizontally and vertically.

Delete the Shell feature.

Maintain the original fillet dimension in the handle of 20mm. Maintain the overall dimension between the two cylinders of 150mm.

Calculate the mass of the part in grams.

Decimal places: 2.

SOLIDWORKS will present multiple views of the model in the question (an overall view of the sketch) or the overall depth of the feature.

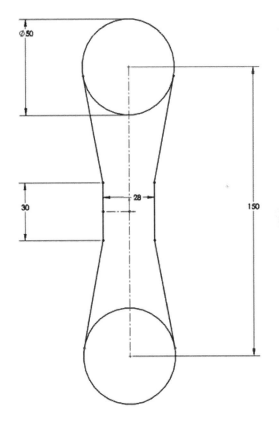

Let's begin. Start with the Sample7-4 model.

1. **Suppress** the Shell1 feature from the FeatureManager. As a general rule, suppress features before you delete them. This will inform you if there are any rebuild or feature errors during modification in the exam.

2. **Edit** Sketch1 (Multi-body sketch) from the Boss-Extrude2 feature in the FeatureManager. View the dimensions. Keep the 150mm dimension.

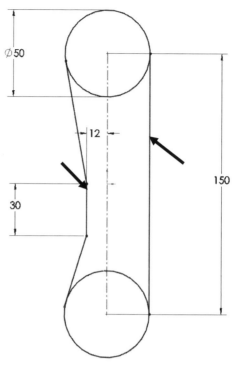

3. **Delete** any unneeded geometric relations (Horizontal) or sketch entities (vertical line) as illustrated. Deleting the Horizontal relation on the point provides the ability to move the attached sketch entities.

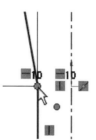

4. **Create** a horizontal centerline between the origin and the midpoint of the vertical line to the left of the origin.

5. **Insert** a Horizontal relation. As a general rule, insert geometric relations before dimensions in a sketch.

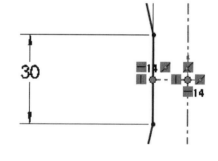

There are numerous ways to address the models in this book. A goal is to display different design intents and techniques for a timed exam.

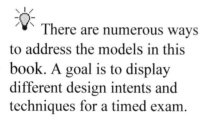

The question was to create a symmetrical handle between the two cylinders. The handle is symmetrical both horizontally and vertically. Add a symmetric relation.

6. **Select** the Centerline, the two end points on the sketch and add a symmetric relation.

Sketch1 is fully defined. Mirror the sketch to the right side.

7. **Window-select** the sketch on the left side and apply the Mirror Entities Sketch tool. Mirror about the vertical centerline. The sketch is fully defined.

The width between the two vertical lines in the initial question displayed a sketch that showed 28mm.

8. **Modify** the 12mm dimension to 14mm to obtain the needed width.

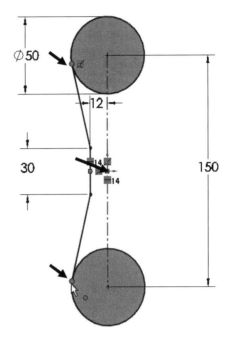

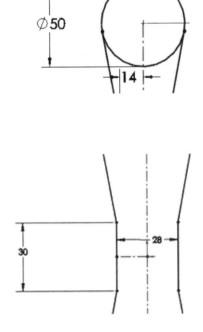

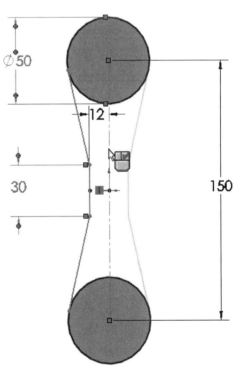

Address all needed fillet features. Maintain the original fillet dimension in the handle of 20mm.

9. **Edit** the Fillet1 feature. Select the two edges. Four edges should be displayed in the Fillet1 PropertyManager.

10. **Calculate** the mass of the part in grams.

11. **Enter 1576.76** grams.

12. **Save** Sample7-4 as Sample7-5.

 SOLIDWORKS Mass Properties calculates the center of mass for every model. At every instant of time, there is a unique location (x, y, z) in space that is the average position of the system's mass. The CSWP exam asks for center of gravity. For the purpose of calculating the center of mass and center of gravity near to earth or on earth, you can assume that the center of mass and the center of gravity are the same.

 Always save your models.

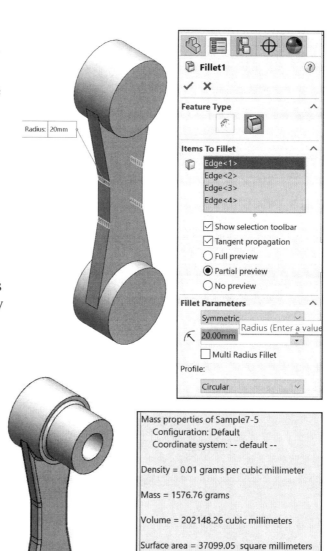

Mass properties of Sample7-5
  Configuration: Default
  Coordinate system: -- default --

Density = 0.01 grams per cubic millimeter

Mass = 1576.76 grams

Volume = 202148.26 cubic millimeters

Surface area = 37099.05 square millimeters

Center of mass: (millimeters)
  X = 8.46
  Y = -6.04
  Z = 0.00

A question in this section could be - modify the depth of the Boss-Extrude3 feature.

Modify the height from 57mm to 47mm. This would mean that the height of the smaller boss is 17mm.

Delete the Shell feature.

Calculate the mass of the part in grams.

Decimal places: 2.

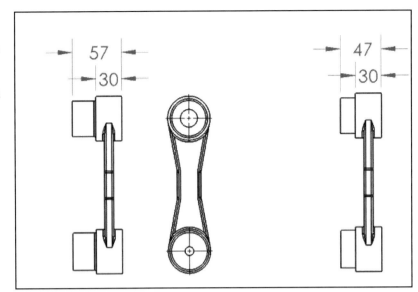

This looks like a straightforward problem. Be careful. SOLIDWORKS wants you to understand how to create features and their options.

Let's begin.

Start with the Sample7-5 model. In Sample7-5, the Shell1 feature is suppress.

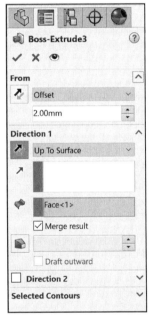

1. **Edit** Boss-Extrude3 from the FeatureManager. Note the sketch is not created from the base of the larger cylinder. The Start Condition is Offset. The End Condition is Up To Surface. The two circular sketches were created on Plane1.

2. **Enter** 2mm (you need 47mm - Offset by 12 - reduce it to 2mm) in the Enter Offset Value box to obtain the needed value.

Confirm that your math is correct. Use the Measure tool during the exam.

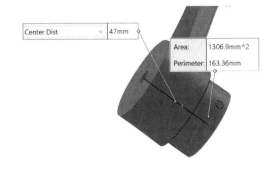

3. **Calculate** the mass of the part in grams.

4. **Enter 1401.30** grams.

5. **Save** Sample7-5 as Sample7-6.

A question in this section could be - modify the sketch on the bottom cylinder to a 21mm square, centered on the cylindrical feature as illustrated.

The square boss contains no fillets.

Maintain all dimensions for both the 10mm and 5mm thru holes as illustrated.

Calculate the mass of the part in grams.

Decimal places: 2.

Think about the feature that you need to delete.

Will there be rebuild errors that you need to address? Yes, there will be in the exam.

Study the provided views and read the question carefully. Remember, there is no partial credit.

Let's begin.

Start with your model Sample7-6.

Delete the original Sketch entities. You need to modify the sketch on the bottom cylinder to a 21mm square, centered on the cylindrical feature.

6. **Edit** Sketch2 from the Boss-Extrude3 feature.

7. **Window-select** the bottom cylinder sketch entities as illustrated.

8. **Press** Delete.

9. **Click** Yes from the SOLIDWORKS dialog box.

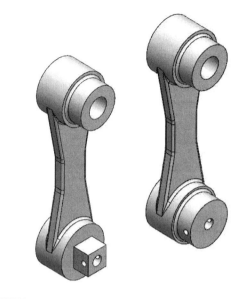

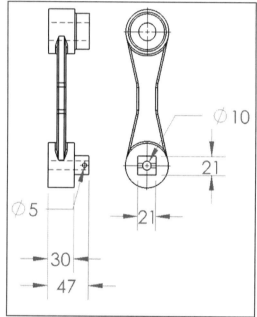

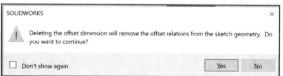

SOLIDWORKS   ×

⚠ Deleting the offset dimension will remove the offset relations from the sketch geometry. Do you want to continue?

☐ Don't show again   [Yes]   [No]

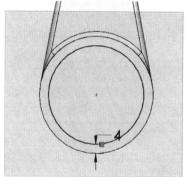

10. **Create** a Center Rectangle sketch located at the center point of the Boss-Extrude1 feature as illustrated.

11. **Insert** needed geometric relations and dimension.

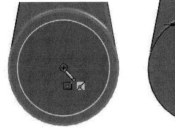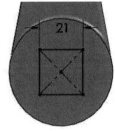

You deleted a circular face to create a square face. A rebuild error is displayed. The sketch contains dimensions or relations to model geometry which no longer exists.

12. **Click** Stop and Repair.

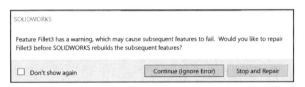

13. **Repair** the Fillet3 feature. You deleted the sketch geometry when you created the center rectangle.

14. **Repair** the Plane2 feature. Plane2 used the small cylindrical face which was deleted. Use the large cylindrical face to repair.

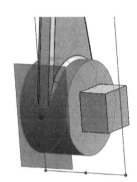

15. **Repair** the Cut-Extrude1 feature. Edit Sketch3. Delete (Coincident1) a dangling sketch entity.

16. **Insert** a Concentric relation to fully define Sketch3. Sketch3 is fully defined. Exit the sketch.

Sketch4 contains dimensions or relations to model geometry which no longer exists. Address Sketch4.

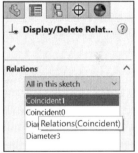

17. **Edit** the Sketch Plane of Sketch4. The original Sketch plane was located on the cylindrical face of Boss-Extrude3 which was modified. Select a new Sketch Plane.

18. A SOLIDWORKS dialog box is displayed. **Press** the Continue (Ignore Error) button.

There are still a few dangling relations associated with the small hole (Cut-Extrude2).

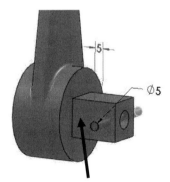

19. **Edit** Sketch4. Delete the Coincident0 and Distance2 relation.

20. **Fully define** Sketch4. Insert the needed dimension and Coincident relation. The hole should be centered on the Boss-Extrude3 feature.

You now have a clean part with no error messages.

21. **Calculate** the mass of the part in grams.

22. **Enter 1278.37** grams.

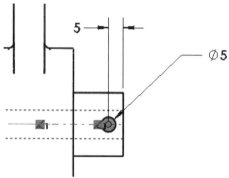

You are finished with the Segment 2 section in this chapter. The questions in the segment are not too difficult, but this is a timed exam. Managing your time is key in any segment of the CSWP CORE exam.

There are numerous ways to address the model in this section. A goal is to display different design intents and techniques.

Always save your models to verify the results.

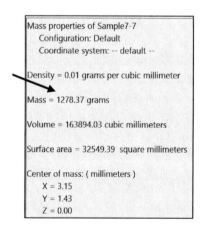

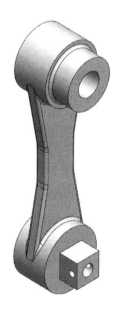

Segment 2 - Additional Practice Problems

In this section, there are fewer step-by-step procedures. Utilize the rollback bar if needed in the provided initial and final models.

Question 1:

A question in this section could be - How many configurations are there associated with this part?

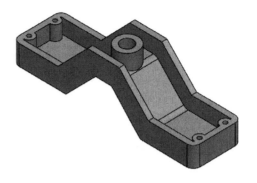

Let's begin.

1. **Open** the CSWP PP 4-1 part from the Segment 2 Initial folder.

2. **Click** the ConfigurationManager tab in the design tree. View the different configurations of the part.

3. **Select 3** for the number of configurations in the multiple-choice answer section of the exam. The first question in this segment is typically in a multiple-choice format.

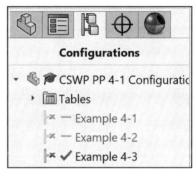

a) 1, b) 2, c) **3**, d) 4

4. **Save** the model.

☀ Double-click on each configuration in the ConfigurationManager. The FeatureManager displays a different material for each configuration. It is important that you understand that these materials will change in the exam and to understand where you would start a new configuration to the existing ConfigurationManager.

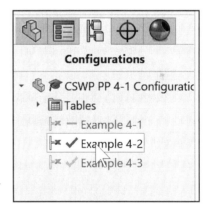

Question 1: Part II

A question in this section could be - calculate the mass in grams of configuration Example 4-2.

Provided Information:

Decimal places: 2.

Let's begin.

1. **Double-click** Example 4-2. Example 4-2 is the active configuration.

2. **Calculate** the mass of the Example 4-2 configuration in grams.

3. **Enter 1229.65** grams for the answer. It is very important to input the proper decimal places as requested in the exam. In this case (2) two.

4. **Save** the model.

Question 3:

A question in this section could be - create a new configuration named Example 4-4 based on the Example 4-3 configuration.

Modify the design table with the specified values.

- D1@Sketch1=70

- D2@Sketch1=50

- D3@Sketch1=46

- D5@Extrude-Thin1=30

- D1@Shell1=8

- D1@Sketch2=12

- Cut-Extrude3=Suppressed

- Cut-Extrude4=Unsuppressed

Calculate the mass of the part (Example 4-4 configuration) in grams.

Decimal places: 2.

Let's begin.

1. **Double-click** the Example 4-3 configuration. This is the active configuration.

2. **Add** a new Configuration, named Example 4-4.

3. **Edit** the Design Table. Modify the design table with the new specified values.

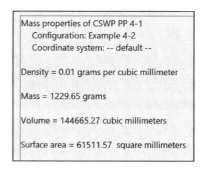

Mass properties of CSWP PP 4-1
Configuration: Example 4-2
Coordinate system: -- default --

Density = 0.01 grams per cubic millimeter

Mass = 1229.65 grams

Volume = 144665.27 cubic millimeters

Surface area = 61511.57 square millimeters

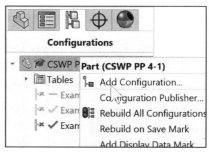

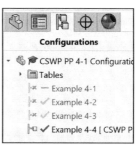

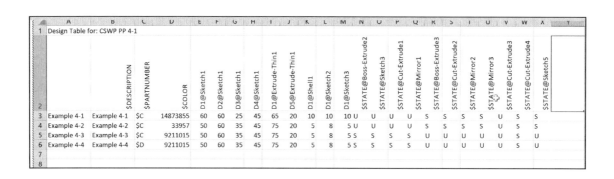

	A	B	C	D	E	F	G	H	I	J	K	L	M	N	O	P	Q	R	S	T	U	V	W	X
1	Design Table for: CSWP PP 4-1																							
2			$DESCRIPTION	$PARTNUMBER	$COLOR	D1@Sketch1	D2@Sketch1	D3@Sketch1	D4@Sketch1	D1@Extrude-Thin1	D5@Extrude-Thin1	D1@Shell1	D1@Sketch2	D1@Sketch3	$STATE@Boss-Extrude2	$STATE@Sketch3	$STATE@Cut-Extrude1	$STATE@Mirror1	$STATE@Boss-Extrude3	$STATE@Cut-Extrude2	$STATE@Mirror2	$STATE@Mirror3	$STATE@Cut-Extrude3	$STATE@Cut-Extrude4	$STATE@Sketch5
3	Example 4-1	Example 4-1	$C	14873855	60	60	25	45	65	20	10	10	10	U	U	U	U	S	S	S	S	U	S	S
4	Example 4-2	Example 4-2	$C	33957	50	60	35	45	75	20	5	8	5	U	U	U	U	S	S	S	U	S	S
5	Example 4-3	Example 4-3	$C	9211015	50	60	35	45	75	20	5	8	5	S	S	S	S	U	U	U	U	S	U
6	Example 4-4	Example 4-4	$D	9211015	50	60	35	45	75	20	5	8	5	S	S	S	S	U	U	U	U	S	U

	$DESCRIPTION	$PARTNUMBER	$COLOR	D1@Sketch1	D2@Sketch1	D3@Sketch1	D4@Sketch1	D1@Extrude-Thin1	D5@Extrude-Thin1	D1@Shell1	D1@Sketch2	D1@Sketch3	$STATE@Boss-Extrude2	$STATE@Sketch3	$STATE@Cut-Extrude1	$STATE@Mirror1	$STATE@Boss-Extrude3	$STATE@Cut-Extrude2	$STATE@Mirror2	$STATE@Mirror3	$STATE@Cut-Extrude3	$STATE@Cut-Extrude4	$STATE@Sketch5
Example 4-1	Example 4-1	$C	14873855	60	60	25	45	65	20	10	10	10	U	U	U	U	S	S	S	S	U	S	S
Example 4-2	Example 4-2	$C	33957	50	60	35	45	75	20	5	8	5	U	U	U	U	S	S	S	S	U	S	S
Example 4-3	Example 4-3	$C	9211015	50	60	35	45	75	20	5	8	5	S	S	S	S	U	U	U	U	U	S	U
Example 4-4	Example 4-4	$D	9211015	70	50	46	45	75	30	8	12	5	S	S	S	S	U	U	U	U	S	U	U

Design Table for: CSWP PP 4-1

4. **Exit** the Design Table.

5. **Calculate** the mass of the part (Example 4-4 configuration) in grams.

6. **Enter 2663.48** grams for the answer. It is very important to input the proper decimal places as requested in the exam.

7. **Save** the part.

Mass properties of CSWP PP 4-1
   Configuration: Example 4-4
   Coordinate system: -- default --

Density = 0.01 grams per cubic millimeter

Mass = 2663.48 grams

Volume = 341471.93 cubic millimeters

Surface area = 93551.54 square millimeters

Center of mass: (millimeters)
   X = 141.00
   Y = -4.95
   Z = 0.00

Segment 2 - Additional Practice Problems

In this section, there are fewer step-by-step procedures. Utilize the rollback bar if needed in the provided initial and final models.

Question 1:

A question in this section could be - modify part CSWP PP5-1 per the provided drawing information.

What is the mass of the new part?

All holes through all unless shown otherwise.

Units: MMGS (millimeters, grams, second)

Decimal Places: 2

Part Origin: Arbitrary

Material: Cast Alloy Steel

Density: 7300 kg/m^2

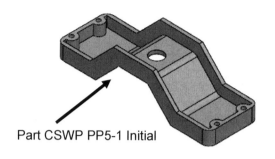

Part CSWP PP5-1 Initial

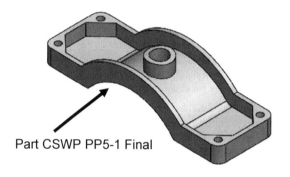

Part CSWP PP5-1 Final

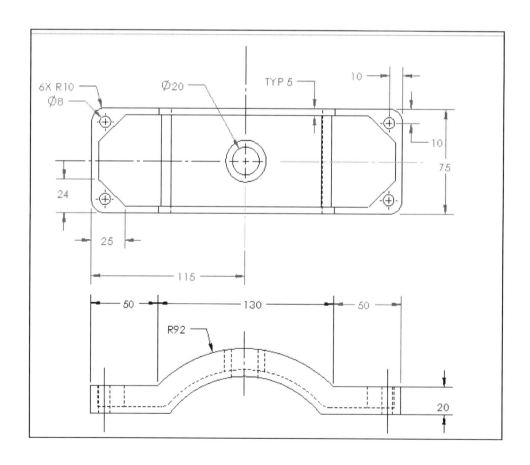

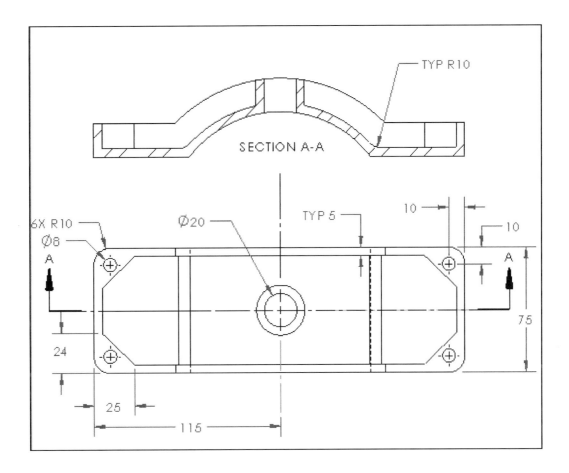

Note: In the exam, the part before modification is labeled 1 and the part after the modification is labeled 2.

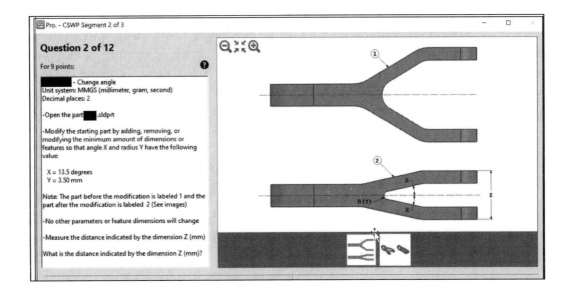

Let's begin.

1. **Create** a folder to save your working model.

2. **Open** the CSWP PP5-1 part from the Segment 2 Initial folder.

3. **View** the FeatureManager.

4. **Use** the Rollbar bar to examine and modify features and sketches from the provided drawing information.

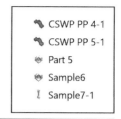

5. **Modify** the Extrude-Thin1 sketch as illustrated using a 3point Arc Sketch tool. Both sketches are fully defined. Dimensions and geometric relations define the sketches. The drawing views provide the needed information for sketch and feature modification of the part.

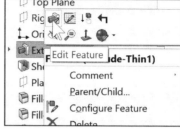

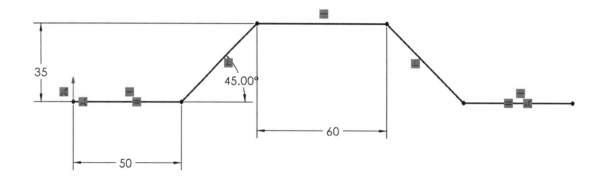

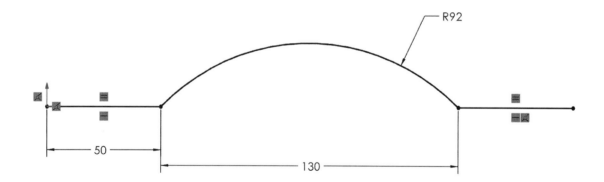

6. **Exit** the sketch. Continue and ignore any errors.

7. **Move** the rollback bar down below the Shell1 feature. Shell1 displays an error in the FeatureManager.

8. **Edit** the Shell feature (Shell1). Remove the missing faces and select the face of the arc to address the error.

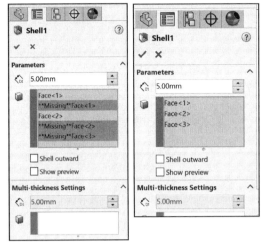

9. **Move** the rollback bar down below the Fillet2 feature. Fillet2 displays an error in the FeatureManager.

10. **Edit** the second Fillet feature (Fillet2). Remove the missing edges and update the edges where the arc and the lines meet as illustrated.

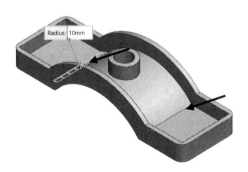

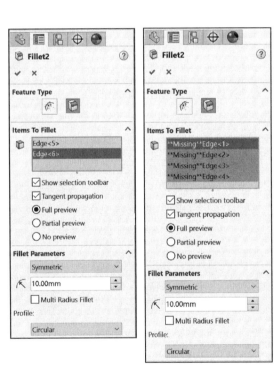

11. **Move** the rollback bar down below the Cut-Extrude4 feature in the FeatureManager. The sketch for Cut-Extrude4 contains dimensions or relations to model geometry which no longer exist.

12. **Edit** the Sketch plane for the Cut-Extrude4 feature. There are missing items in the feature. Remove the missing plane.

13. **Select** Top Plane for the sketch plane. Remember the provided drawing information. An Extruded-Cut feature is needed on the top of the arc.

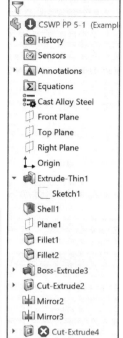

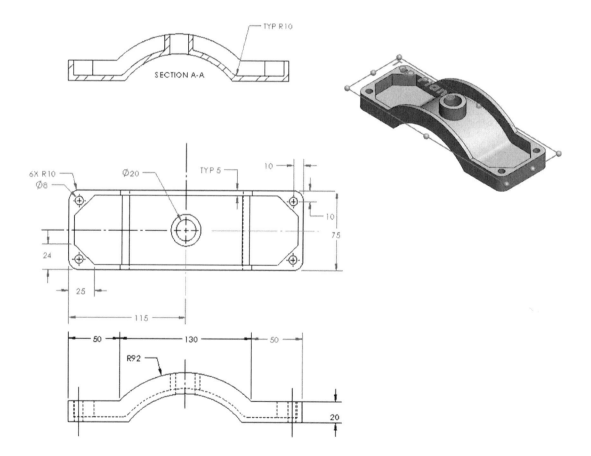

SECTION A-A

TYP R10

6X R10
Ø8

Ø20

TYP 5

R92

14. **Continue** and ignore any errors. **Close** the What's Wrong dialog box.

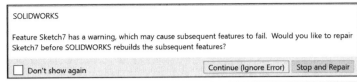

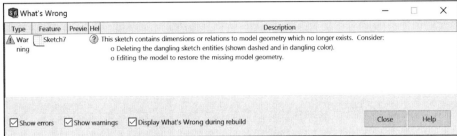

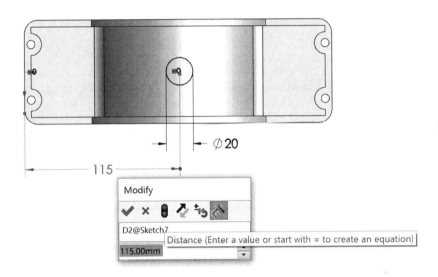

15. **Center** the hole on the part as illustrated. Delete the midpoint relation and add a dimension of 115mm from the center of the hole to the side edge of the part.

16. **Move** the Cut-Extrude4 feature before the Shell1 feature in the FeatureManager as illustrated.

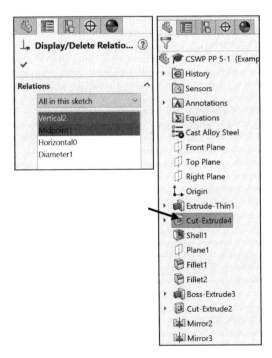

17. **View** the results in the Graphics window.

18. **Edit** the Boss-Extrude3 sketch (Sketch4). Modify the sketch per the provided information in the drawing.

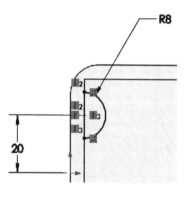

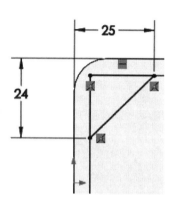

19. **Continue** and ignore any errors. Close the What's Wrong dialog box.

20. **Edit** Sketch5. Modify the location of the center hole. Delete the Coincident relation with the center of the circle. Drag the center of the circle so that it is Coincident with the center of the corner fillet.

21. **Modify** the diameter of the hole from 6mm to 8mm. Exit the Sketch.

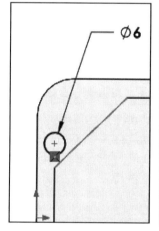

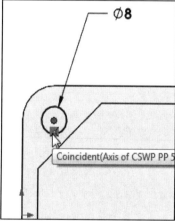

22. **Calculate** the mass of the part in grams.

23. **Enter 1088.85** grams.

24. **Save** the part.

You are finished with this section. Good luck on the exam.

There are numerous ways to build the model in this section. A goal is to display different design intents and techniques.

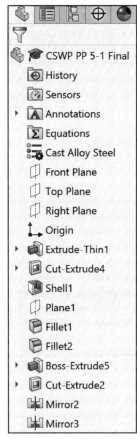

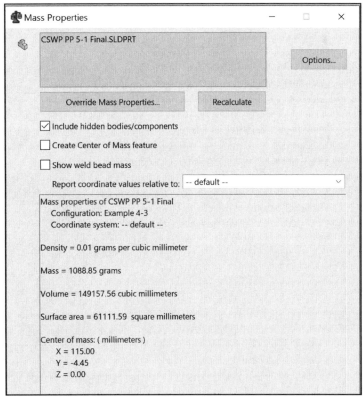

Below are former screen shots from a previous CSWP exam in Segment 2.

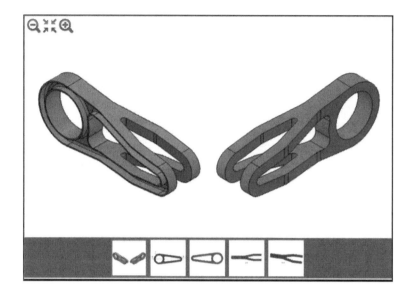

Unit system: MMGS (millimeter, gram, second)
Decimal places: 2

-Open the pa███████.sldprt

-Modify the starting part by adding, removing, or modifying the minimum amount of dimensions or features so that angle X and radius Y have the following value:

   X = 14.5 degrees
   Y = 2.50 mm

Note: The part before the modification is labeled 1 and the part after the modification is labeled 2 (See images)

-No other parameters or feature dimensions will change

-Measure the distance indicated by the dimension Z (mm)

What is the distance indicated by the dimension Z (mm)?

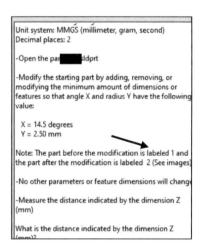

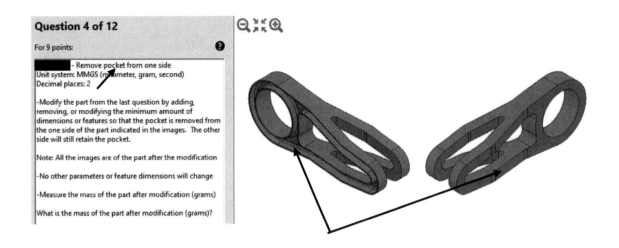

Question 4 of 12

For 9 points:

[ ] - Remove pocket from one side
Unit system: MMGS (millimeter, gram, second)
Decimal places: 2

-Modify the part from the last question by adding, removing, or modifying the minimum amount of dimensions or features so that the pocket is removed from the one side of the part indicated in the images. The other side will still retain the pocket.

Note: All the images are of the part after the modification

-No other parameters or feature dimensions will change

-Measure the mass of the part after modification (grams)

What is the mass of the part after modification (grams)?

If your school is an academic certification provider, your instructor can allocate a free exam credit for the CSWP - Segment 1, Segment 2 or Segment 3. The instructor will require your .edu email address.

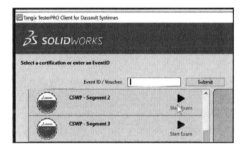

Notes:

CHAPTER 3 - SEGMENT 3 OF THE CSWP CORE EXAM

Introduction

Segment 3 is 80 minutes long with fourteen (14) questions divided into three categories.

Segment 3 focuses on assemblies and modifications.

Download the .zip folder. The .zip folder contains the needed parts for this segment.

The format is either multiple-choice or single fill in the blank.

A total score of 77 out of 109 or better is required to pass.

Segment 3 requires knowledge of the following:

- Create an assembly

- Insert downloaded components and sub-assemblies

- Assembly and mate parts in an assembly

- Utilize Standard & Advanced (Width, Distance, Angle, etc.) mates

- Measure angles

- Mate modification

- Suppress mates

- Move/Rotate components

- Apply Rigid and Flexible states

- Employ the Interference Detection and Collision tools

- Create and use a new Coordinate System

- Modify and replace components

- Recover from mate errors

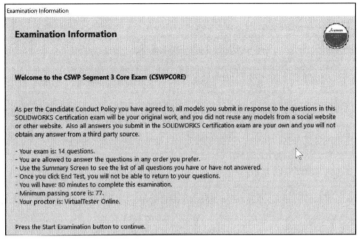

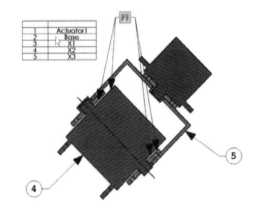

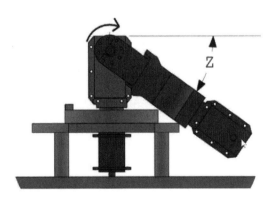

- Calculate mass and center of mass

- Recognize Engineering drawing views with annotations

Question 1: Instructional page. Read the instructions. Agree to the Candidate Conduct Policy. Click Yes.

Click the link to download the needed components, sub-assemblies and assemblies.

Save the downloaded files to a working folder, (Extract All).

Click Next Question.

Question 2: Multiple-choice format. Create a new assembly. Insert a part. Create a new Coordinate system.

Use the Mass Properties tool. You should be within 0.5% of the stated value in the multiple-choice section before you go to the next question. There is no partial credit.

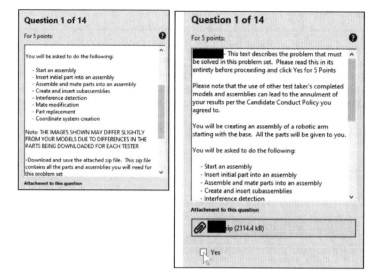

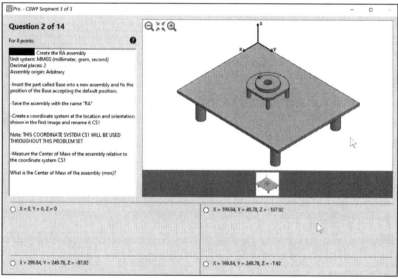

During the exam, you will be asked to refer to various images, to ensure that you have the correct orientation and the assembly is fully constrained.

Note: If you fail this segment of the exam, you need to wait 14 days before you can retake it. In that time, you can take another segment.

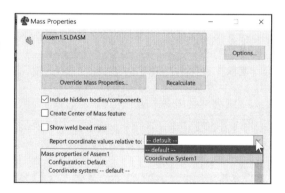

Question 3: Single fill in the blank format. During the exam, you will be forced into an error situation. Decimal place 2. Units: MMGS.

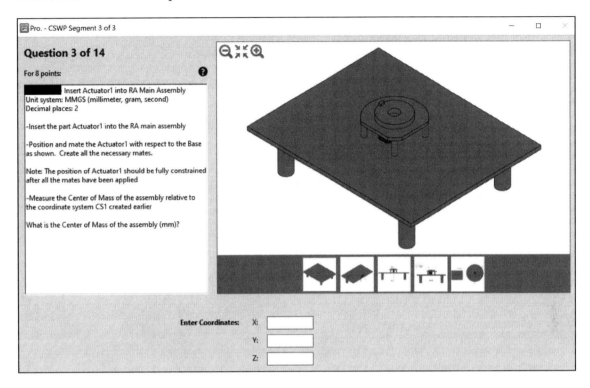

Question 4: Single fill in the blank format. You are still working on the same assembly.

Decimal places: 2. Units: MMGS.

Question 5: Multiple-choice format. You should be within 0.5% of the stated value in the multiple-choice section before you go to the next question. There is no partial credit.

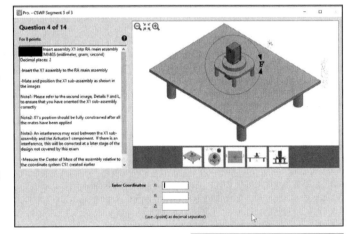

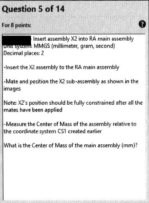

Question 6: Single fill in the blank format.

You are requested to use Collision Detection and measure an angle within 0.10 degrees. Remember Decimal places: 2.

Question 7: Single fill in the blank format. Create a new assembly. Take your time. This is a new assembly.

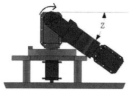
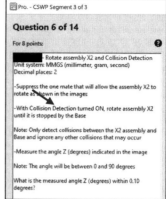

Question 6 of 14

For 8 points:

- Rotate assembly X2 and Collision Detection
Unit system: MMGS (millimeter, gram, second)
Decimal places: 2

-Suppress the one mate that will allow the assembly X2 to rotate as shown in the images

-With Collision Detection turned ON, rotate assembly X2 until it is stopped by the Base

Note: Only detect collisions between the X2 assembly and Base and ignore any other collisions that may occur

-Measure the angle Z (degrees) indicated in the image

Note: The angle will be between 0 and 90 degrees

What is the measured angle Z (degrees) within 0.10 degrees?

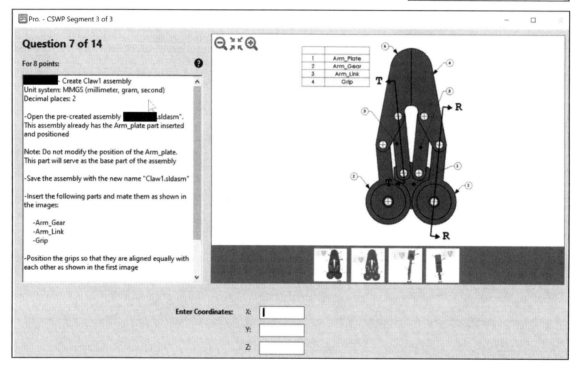

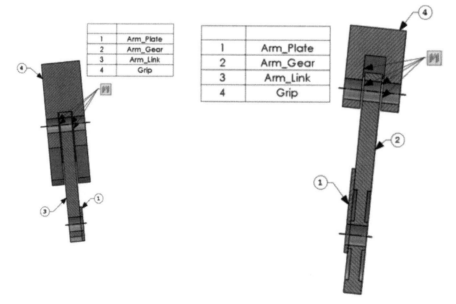

Question 8: Multiple-choice format. You should be within 0.5% of the stated value in the multiple-choice section before you go to the next question. There is no partial credit.

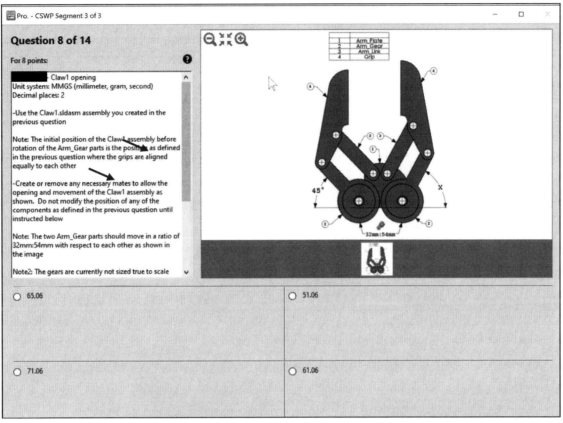

Question 8 of 14

For 8 points:

- Claw1 opening
Unit system: MMGS (millimeter, gram, second)
Decimal places: 2

-Use the Claw1.sldasm assembly you created in the previous question

Note: The initial position of the Claw1 assembly before rotation of the Arm_Gear parts is the position as defined in the previous question where the grips are aligned equally to each other

-Create or remove any necessary mates to allow the opening and movement of the Claw1 assembly as shown. Do not modify the position of any of the components as defined in the previous question until instructed below

Note: The two Arm_Gear parts should move in a ratio of 32mm:54mm with respect to each other as shown in the image

Note2: The gears are currently not sized true to scale

○ 65.06   ○ 51.06

○ 71.06   ○ 61.06

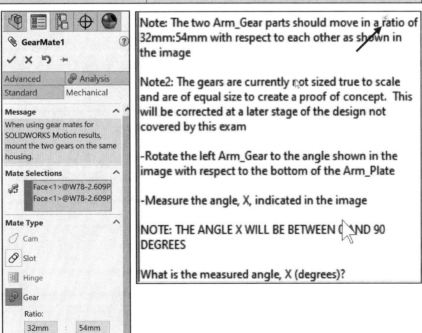

GearMate1

Note: The two Arm_Gear parts should move in a ratio of 32mm:54mm with respect to each other as shown in the image

Note2: The gears are currently not sized true to scale and are of equal size to create a proof of concept. This will be corrected at a later stage of the design not covered by this exam

-Rotate the left Arm_Gear to the angle shown in the image with respect to the bottom of the Arm_Plate

-Measure the angle, X, indicated in the image

NOTE: THE ANGLE X WILL BE BETWEEN 0 AND 90 DEGREES

What is the measured angle, X (degrees)?

Question 9: Single fill in the blank format. Open a new assembly.

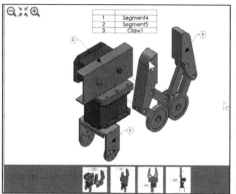

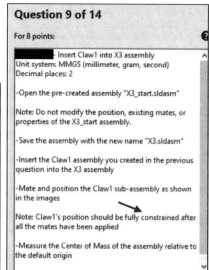

Question 9 of 14

For 8 points:

_____ - Insert Claw1 into X3 assembly
Unit system: MMGS (millimeter, gram, second)
Decimal places: 2

-Open the pre-created assembly "X3_start.sldasm"

Note: Do not modify the position, existing mates, or properties of the X3_start assembly.

-Save the assembly with the new name "X3.sldasm"

-Insert the Claw1 assembly you created in the previous question into the X3 assembly

-Mate and position the Claw1 sub-assembly as shown in the images

Note: Claw1's position should be fully constrained after all the mates have been applied

-Measure the Center of Mass of the assembly relative to the default origin

Question 10: Multiple-choice format. You should be within 0.5% of the stated value in the multiple-choice section before you go to the next question. There is no partial credit.

Return to an assembly.

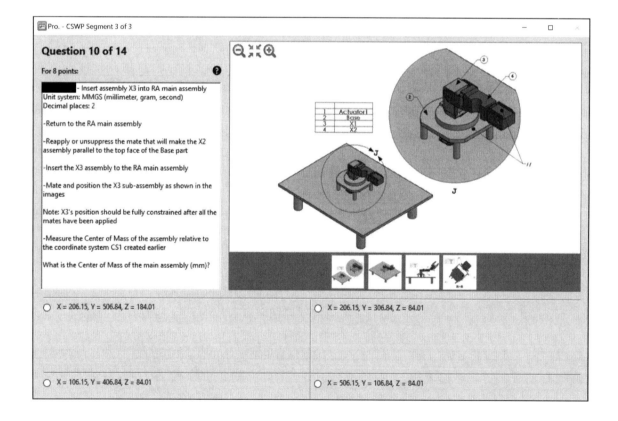

Question 10 of 14

For 8 points:

_____ - Insert assembly X3 into RA main assembly
Unit system: MMGS (millimeter, gram, second)
Decimal places: 2

-Return to the RA main assembly

-Reapply or unsuppress the mate that will make the X2 assembly parallel to the top face of the Base part

-Insert the X3 assembly to the RA main assembly

-Mate and position the X3 sub-assembly as shown in the images

Note: X3's position should be fully constrained after all the mates have been applied

-Measure the Center of Mass of the assembly relative to the coordinate system CS1 created earlier

What is the Center of Mass of the main assembly (mm)?

○ X = 206.15, Y = 506.84, Z = 184.01

○ X = 206.15, Y = 306.84, Z = 84.01

○ X = 106.15, Y = 406.84, Z = 84.01

○ X = 506.15, Y = 106.84, Z = 84.01

Question 11: Single fill in the blank format. Return to a sub-assembly. Modify the sub-assembly. Then return to the main assembly.

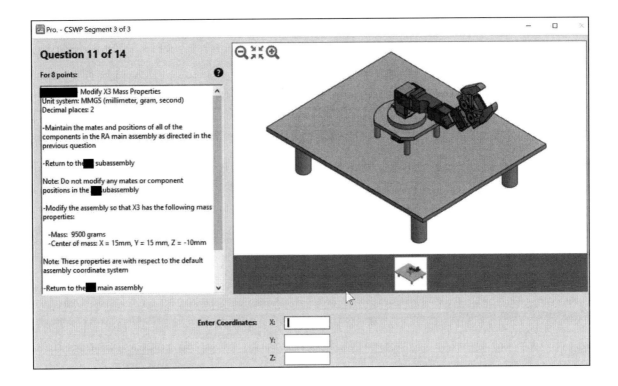

Question 12: Multiple-choice format.

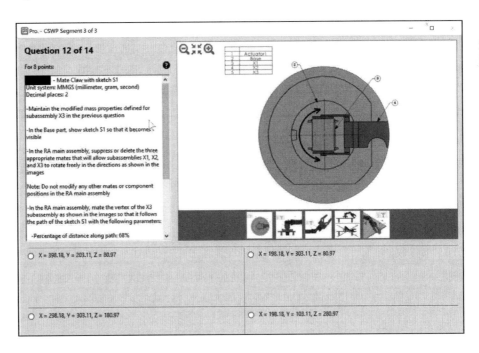

Question 13: Single fill in the blank format. In the exam, it may state: Roll Control: Free. Pitch/Yaw Control: Free. This means you can rotate freely about X, Y, and Z in the assembly.

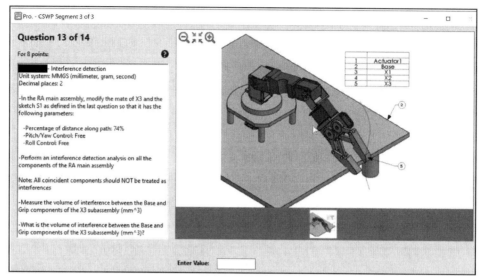

Question 14: Single fill in the blank format.

There are numerous ways to address the question in this section. A goal is to display different design intents and techniques.

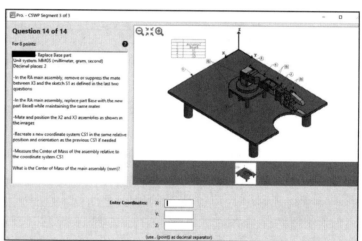

Segment 3 of the CSWP Core Exam

Create an assembly (Welding Arm) starting with the Base1 component. Some components in the exam are modeled by you and others will be supplied to you.

Load the Testing client and read the instructions. Create a folder to save your working models.

The first question is an instructional page. Read the instructions. Agree to the Candidate Conduct Policy. Click Yes. It's a free 5 points.

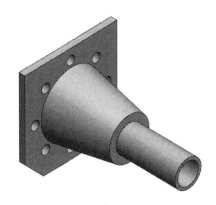

Download the needed components, sub-assemblies and assemblies. Save the downloaded files to a working folder, (Extract All). Click Next Question.

The second question can be - Create the Base1 part.

Calculate the mass of the Base1 part in grams.

Information on the Base1 part is provided to you in a variety of drawing views.

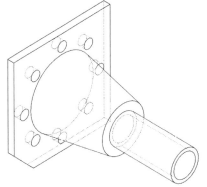

Provided information:

Unit system: MMGS (millimeter, gram, second)

Decimal place: 2

Material of Base1: Cast Stainless Steel

Density: 0.0077 g/m^3

Part origin: Arbitrary

All holes through all unless shown otherwise.

Note: Base1 is displayed in an Isometric view.

View 1:

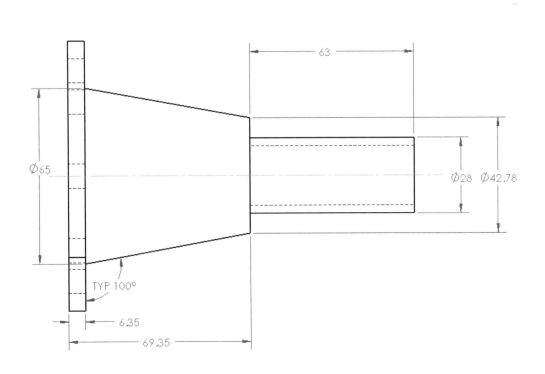

View 2:

Details are very important. Note the location of the top seed feature (Cut-Extrude1) located along the Y-axis in the drawing view. The Chamfer feature is located in the lower corner. This is important when you insert the Base1 component into the assembly document to calculate the center of gravity relative to the specified coordinate system location.

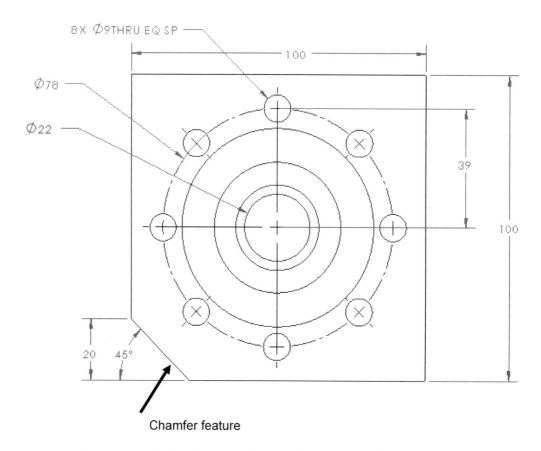

Chamfer feature

Take your time to first identify the drawing views and to better understand the provided geometry that is needed to create the initial part.

There are numerous ways to build this model.

The images displayed on the exam are not to scale due to differences in the parts being downloaded for each tester.

🔆 Download all needed model files (initial and final) and the SOLIDWORKS CSWP Sample Exam folder from the SDC Publications website (www.SDCpublications.com/downloads/978-1-63057-542-7).

🔆 If your school is an academic certification provider, your instructor can allocate a free exam credit for the CSWP (Segment 1, Segment 2 or Segment 3). The instructor will require your .edu email address.

Let's begin.

Create the Base1 part. View the provided model and drawing information for dimensions and material type. Set document units and precision. The first component in an assembly should be fixed to the origin or fully defined.

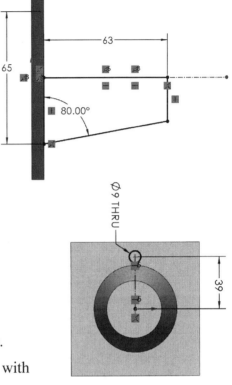

1. **Create** a folder to save your working models.

2. **Set** document properties.

3. **Create** Sketch1 for Base1 on the Right Plane.

4. **Create** the Extruded Base (6.35 Depth) feature.

5. **Apply** material type, Cast Stainless Steel.

6. **Create** the Revolve1 feature using Sketch2 on the Front Plane (69.35mm - 6.35mm).

7. **Create** the first Extruded Cut feature (seed) for the circular pattern.

8. **Create** the Circular pattern (8 Instances) feature.

9. **Create** the Boss-Extrude feature (63mm Depth) with the needed sketch relations and dimensions.

10. **Create** the Chamfer feature.

11. **Calculate** the mass in grams.

12. **Select 1690.78** grams in the multiple-choice answer section of the exam. The first question in this segment is typically in a multiple-choice format.

13. **Save** the part. Name it Base1.

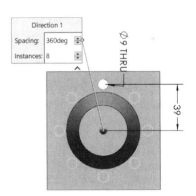

It is good practice to save frequently and to rename the part or assembly if you need to go back during the exam.

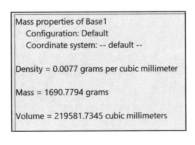

Mass properties of Base1
    Configuration: Default
    Coordinate system: -- default --

Density = 0.0077 grams per cubic millimeter

Mass = 1690.7794 grams

Volume = 219581.7345 cubic millimeters

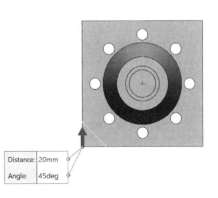

A question in this segment could be - create an Assembly document from the Base1 component.

Calculate the center of gravity in mm of the assembly relative to the new coordinate system (Coordinate System1).

Provided Information:

Unit system: MMGS (millimeter, gram, second)

Decimal places: 2

Assembly origin: Arbitrary

Orientate the Base1 component as illustrated. Create a coordinate system in the lower left corner vertex of the Base1 component as illustrated. Use this coordinate system throughout the problem set.

Let's begin.

1. **Create** an assembly document and insert the Base1 part. By default, the Base1 component is fixed to the origin.

There are numerous ways to modify the orientation of a component in an assembly document that is fixed to the origin.

Use the Float and Mate tools in the next section. Re-orientate the Base1 component as needed. Fully define the component in the Assembly document.

2. **Float** the part. The part is free to translate or rotate in the Assembly document (six degrees of freedom).

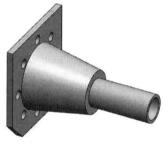

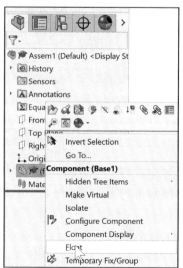

3. **Re-orientate** the assembly as needed. Create a Coincident mate between the Top Plane of the Assembly and the top face of the Base1 component.

4. **Click** the Aligned option.

The Chamfer feature is located in the wrong corner.

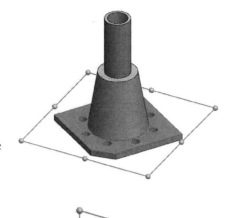

5. **Create** a Coincident mate between the Front Plane of the Assembly and the Top Plane of the Base1 component. The Base1 component is able to translate along the X axis.

Another mate is needed to fully define the component.

6. **Create** a Coincident mate between the Right Plane of the Assembly and the Front Plane of the Base1 component. The Base1 component is fully defined in the Assembly document with three Coincident mates.

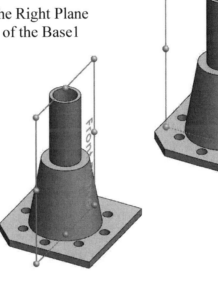

🔆 You can also rotate the Base1 component in the assembly using the Rotate Component tool (about Y & X).

Create the coordinate system to calculate the center of mass for the assembly.

7. **Click** the Coordinate System tool from the Reference Geometry drop-down menu. The Coordinate System PropertyManager is displayed.

8. **Click** the lower front right vertex for the origin. Note the position of X, Y, Z.

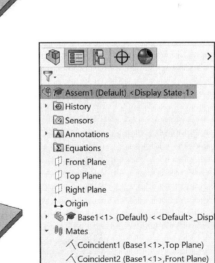

9. **Click** the bottom front edge for the X axis.

10. **Click** the bottom right edge for the Y axis. View the new coordinate system.

11. **Calculate** the center of mass relative to the new coordinate system (Coordinate System1).

12. **Enter** the center of mass (mm) in the three blank fields. You need to be within .5% of the answer to get this question correct.

    X = -49.75

    Y = 50.25

    Z = 29.96

13. **Save** the assembly. In this example name the assembly Welding Arm.

14. **Close** the assembly. In the next section use the downloaded components and assemblies located in the Segment 3 Initial/Initial 2 folder.

Note: You can use your Welding Arm which you created in this section and replace the Welding Arm in the Segment 3 Initial/Initial 2 folder.

 There are numerous ways to build the model in this section. A goal is to display different design intents and techniques.

 If your school is an academic certification provider, your instructor can allocate a free exam credit for the CSWP (Segment 1, Segment 2 or Segment 3). The instructor will require your .edu email address.

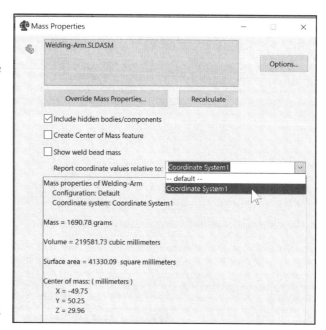

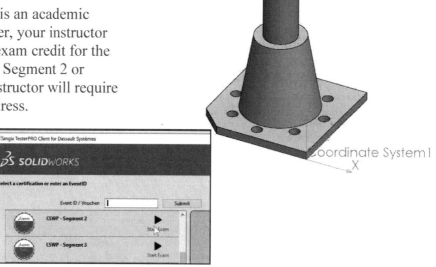

A question in this segment could be - download and open the attached assemblies. Note: All components and assemblies are located in the Segment 3 Initial/Initial 2 folder.

Insert them into the Welding Arm assembly. Position the assemblies (Arm and TopFixture-A) with respect to the Base1 component as illustrated.

Create all required mates.

Calculate the center of mass in mm of the Welding Arm assembly utilizing the created coordinate system (Coordinate System1).

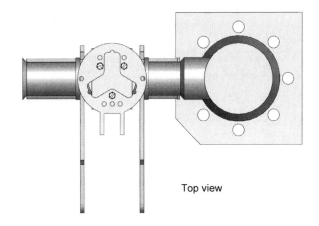

Top view

Imported components have imported geometry. Select "No" on Feature Recognition. Import the geometry as quickly as possible.

Provided Information:

Unit system: MMGS (millimeter, gram, second)

Decimal places: 2

SOLIDWORKS provides symbols to indicate a Parallel mate, Width mate, Coincident mate, etc. in the exam. Take your time to review the drawing views and to understand the required mates between each component.

In this example a Parallel mate is needed between the Front Plane of the Arm sub-assembly and the front narrow face of the Base1 component.

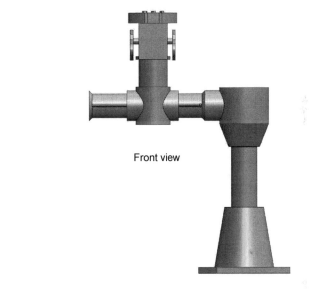

Front view

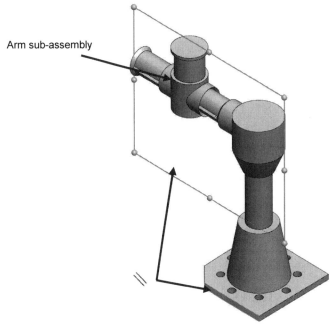

Arm sub-assembly

A Parallel mate is also needed between the right flat face of the TopFixture-A assembly and the right narrow face of the Base1 component.

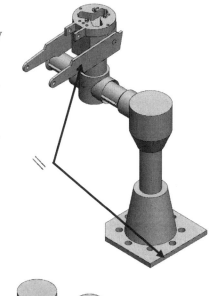

Let's begin.

Open the Welding-Arm assembly. Insert the Arm assembly. Insert two Concentric mates to have the Arm free to rotate about the Base1 component. All components and assemblies are located in the Segment 3 Initial/Initial 2 folder.

1. **Open** the Welding-Arm assembly.

2. **Insert** the Arm assembly (from the Segment 3 Initial/Initial 2 folder) into the Welding Arm assembly.

3. **Insert** a Concentric mate between the outside cylindrical face of the Arm/base2-1 and the inside cylindrical face of Base1.

4. **Insert** a Coincident mate between the bottom inside flat face of Base1 and the bottom face of Arm.

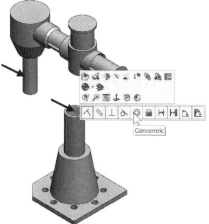

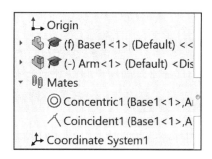

The Arm is free to rotate about the Base1 component. Next orientate the Arm parallel with the front narrow face of the Base1 component. Planes will be used in this section.

5. **Insert** a Parallel mate 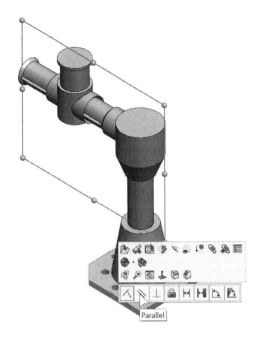 between the Front Plane of the Arm and the front narrow face of Base1.

6. **Click** the Anti-Aligned option for proper position if needed.

Next insert the TopFixture-A assembly into the Welding Arm assembly.

7. **Insert** the TopFixture-A assembly (from the Segment 3 Initial/Initial 2 folder) into the Welding Arm assembly.

8. **Insert** a Coincident mate between the bottom face of TopFixture-A and the top face of the Arm.

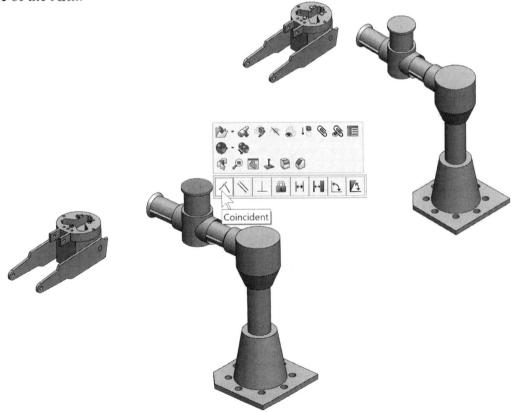

9. **Insert** a Concentric mate between the cylindrical face of the Arm and the cylindrical face of TopFixture-A as illustrated. TopFixture-A is free to rotate in the Welding Arm assembly.

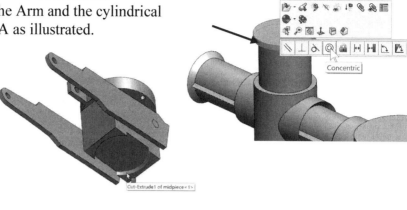

10. **Insert** a Parallel ⬉ mate between the right flat face of the TopFixture-A and the right narrow face of Base1.

11. **Calculate** the center of mass (mm) relative to the new coordinate system.

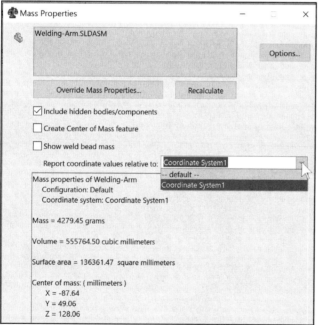

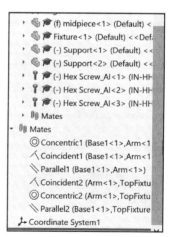

Mass Properties			—		×

Welding-Arm.SLDASM

Options...

Override Mass Properties...   Recalculate

☑ Include hidden bodies/components

☐ Create Center of Mass feature

☐ Show weld bead mass

Report coordinate values relative to: | Coordinate System1 |
-- default --
Coordinate System1

Mass properties of Welding-Arm
  Configuration: Default
  Coordinate system: Coordinate System1

Mass = 4279.45 grams

Volume = 555764.50 cubic millimeters

Surface area = 136361.47 square millimeters

Center of mass: (millimeters)
  X = -87.64
  Y = 49.06
  Z = 128.06

FeatureManager tree:
▸ 🔩 (f) midpiece<1> (Default) <
▸ 🔩 Fixture<1> (Default) < <Def.
▸ 🔩 (-) Support<1> (Default) <<
▸ 🔩 (-) Support<2> (Default) <<
▸ 🔩 (-) Hex Screw_Al<1> (IN-HH
▸ 🔩 (-) Hex Screw_Al<2> (IN-HH
▸ 🔩 (-) Hex Screw_Al<3> (IN-HH
▸ 🔩 Mates
▾ 🔩 Mates
    ◎ Concentric1 (Base1<1>,Arm<1
    ⟍ Coincident1 (Base1<1>,Arm<1
    ⬉ Parallel1 (Base1<1>,Arm<1>)
    ⟍ Coincident2 (Arm<1>,TopFixtu
    ◎ Concentric2 (Arm<1>,TopFixtu
    ⬉ Parallel2 (Base1<1>,TopFixture
  ⤴ Coordinate System1

12. **Enter** the center of mass (mm) in the three blank fields.

    X = -87.64

    Y = 49.06

    Z = 128.06

13. **Save** the assembly.

SOLIDWORKS Mass Properties calculates the center of mass for every model. At every instant of time, there is a unique location (x, y, z) in space that is the average position of the system's mass.

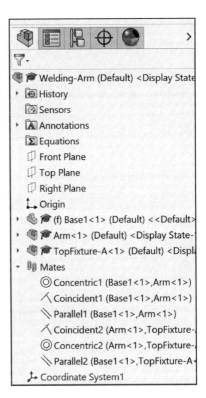

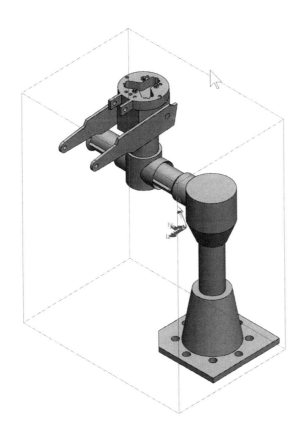

A question in this segment could be - insert the Holder-Thongs-A assembly in the Welding Arm assembly. Insert all needed mates. With Collision Detection turned ON, rotate Holder-Thong-A until Thong is stopped by the Arm-2/Base3-1. Calculate the angle between the flat face of Boss-Extrude1 of the Fixture and the flat face of Boss-Extrude1 of the Holder.

Provided Information:

Unit system: MMGS (millimeter, gram, second)

Decimal places: 2

Knowledge of Collision Detection and the Measure tool is required for this section.

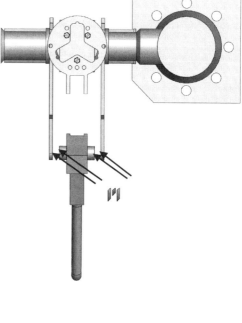

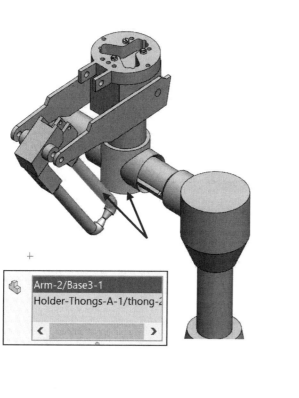

Arm-2/Base3-1
Holder-Thongs-A-1/thong-2

Face<1>@TopFixture-A-1/Fixture-1
Face<2>@Holder-Thongs-A-1/HOLDER-1

Let's begin.

1. **Insert** the Holder-Thongs-A assembly (from the Segment 3 Initial/Initial 3 folder) into the Welding Arm assembly.

2. **Insert** a Concentric mate between the inside cylindrical face of Holder-Thongs-A and the inside cylindrical face of the TopFixture.

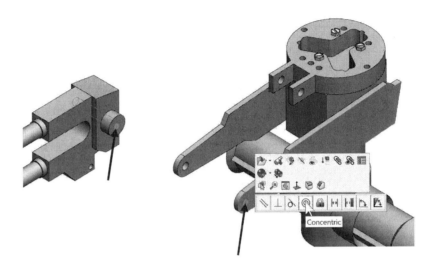

3. **Insert** a Width 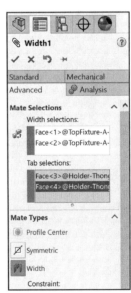 mate between Holder-Thongs-A and TopFixture. The Holder is free to rotate.

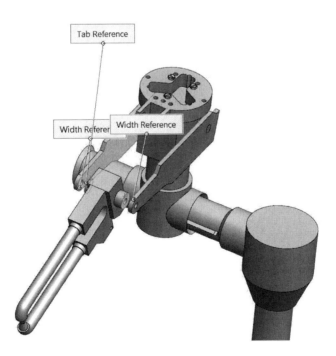

4. **Activate** Collision detection from the Rotate Component PropertyManager.

5. **Rotate** Holder-Thong-A until Thong is stopped by the Arm assembly.

6. **Calculate** the angle between the flat face of Boss-Extrude1 of the Fixture and flat face of Boss-Extrude1 of the Holder.

7. **Enter 144.84**. It is important to input the proper decimal places as requested in the exam.

8. **Save** the assembly. You will need it later in the exam. Note at this time the mass of the assembly is 4561.78 grams.

A question in this segment could be - Decrease the angle between the flat face of Boss-Extrude1 of the Fixture and the flat face of Boss-Extrude1 of the Holder to 144.00 deg. Measure the volume of interference between the Arm-2/Base3-1 and the Holder-Thongs-A-1/thong-2.

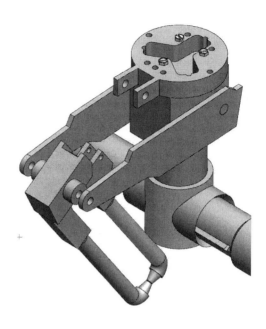

Face<1>@TopFixture-A-1/Fixture-1
Face<2>@Holder-Thongs-A-1/HOLDER-1

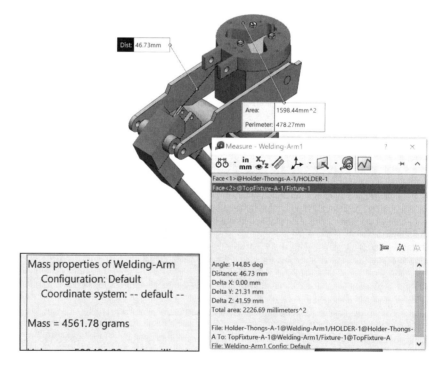

Mass properties of Welding-Arm
   Configuration: Default
   Coordinate system: -- default --

Mass = 4561.78 grams

9. **Decrease** the angle between the flat face of Boss-Extrude1 of the Fixture and the flat face of Boss-Extrude1 of the Holder to 143.00 degrees.

10. **Activate** the Interference Detection tool. View the PropertyManager. Clear all selections. Select the entire Welding Arm assembly.

11. **Enter** - 60.00mm^3

Depending on the angle of rotation of the Holder-Thongs-Assembly the components that interfere will be different.

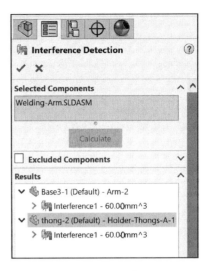

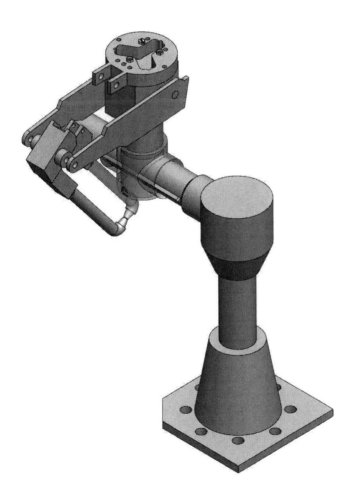

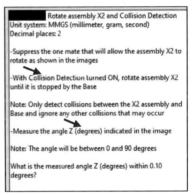

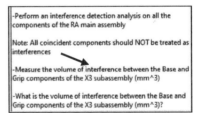

Sample exam questions

A question in this segment could be - Create the Hydraulic and Brace Assembly.

The Hydraulic and Brace Assembly consist of two components: Hydraulic1 & BRACE.

Insert a 20mm Distance mate between the bottom cylindrical face of BRACE and the bottom cylindrical face of Hydraulic1.

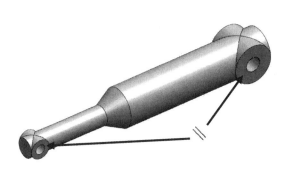

Calculate the mass of the assembly in grams. Save the assembly.

Later insert the assembly into the Welder Arm assembly.

Provided Information:

Unit system: MMGS (millimeter, gram, second)

Decimal places: 2

Material of components: Cast Stainless Steel

Density = 0.0077 g/m^3

Part origin: Arbitrary

Utilize the model folders to follow along while using the book.

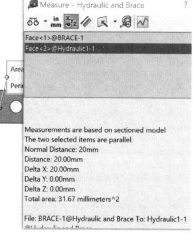

Let's begin.

1. **Create** the Hydraulic and Brace assembly document.

2. **Set** document properties (drafting standard, units and precision).

3. **Insert** the Hydraulic1 component (Segment 3 Initial/Initial 4 folder). The Hydraulic1 component is fixed to the origin.

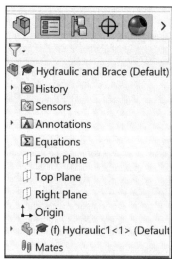

4. **Insert** the BRACE component.

5. **Create** a Concentric mate between the inside cylindrical face of Hydraulic1 and the outside cylindrical face of BRACE.

6. **Create** a Parallel mate between the outside cylindrical face of Hydraulic1 and the outside cylindrical face of BRACE.

7. **Create** a Distance mate (20mm) between the inside bottom face of Hydraulic1 and the bottom flat face of BRACE as illustrated.

8. **Calculate** the mass of the assembly in grams.

9. **Enter 51.55** grams. Always enter the needed decimal places.

10. **Save** the assembly.

Mass properties of Hydraulic and Brace
  Configuration: Default
  Coordinate system: -- default --

Mass = 51.55 grams

Volume = 6694.94 cubic millimeters

A question in this segment could be - Insert the Hydraulic and Brace assembly into the Welding Arm assembly.

Suppress the Distance mate in the Hydraulic and Brace assembly.

Make the Hydraulic and Brace assembly flexible.

Mate and position the Hydraulic and Brace assembly in the Welding Arm assembly.

Set the proper faces (mates) as indicated in the images.

Insert a Width mate to properly position the Hydraulic and Brace assembly in between the mounting holes.

Insert an Angle mate of 25 degrees between the Holder-Thongs-A assembly and the TopFixture-A assembly.

Calculate the mass in grams of the Welding Arm assembly.

Another question could be - calculate the center of mass (mm) relative to Coordinate System1.

Provided Information:

Unit system: MMGS (millimeter, gram, second)

Decimal places: 2

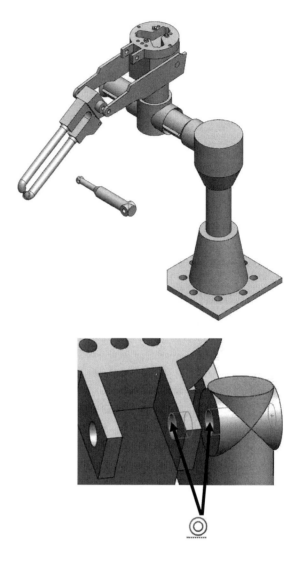

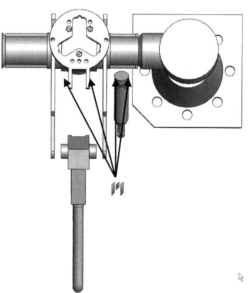

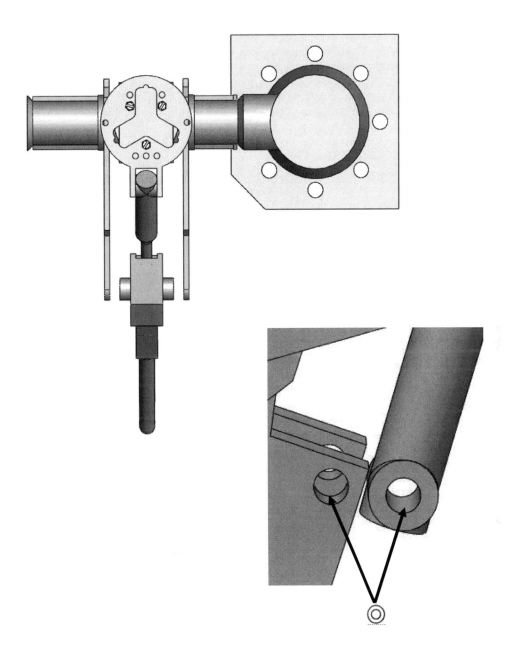

Hydraulic and
Brace assembly

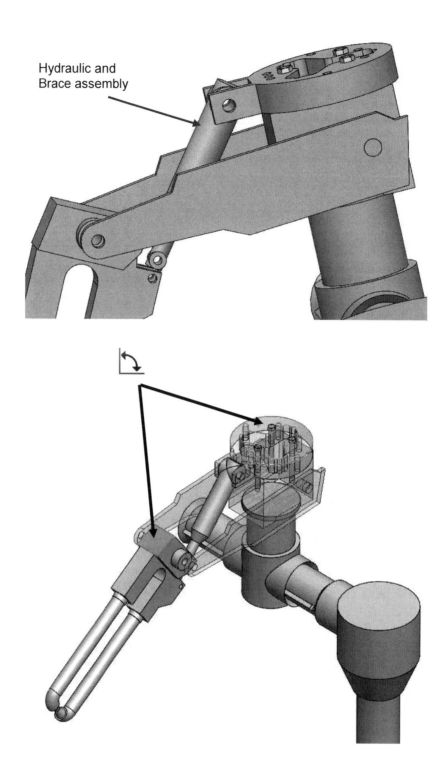

Let's begin.

1. **Insert** the Hydraulic and Brace assembly into the Welding Arm assembly.

2. **Suppress** the Distance mate in the Hydraulic and Brace assembly.

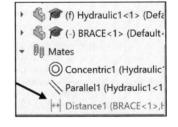

3. **Create** a Concentric mate between the inside cylindrical face of the Hydraulic and Brace assembly and the inside cylindrical face of the Fixture tab.

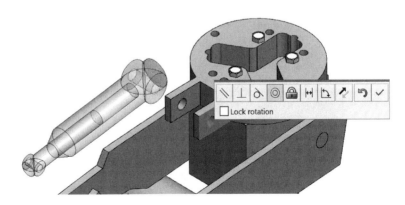

4. **Create** a Width mate between the two tabs (outside faces) of the Fixture and the two outside cylindrical faces of Hydraulic1. The Hydraulic and Brace assembly is free to rotate. When a sub-assembly is inserted into an assembly it is in the rigid state.

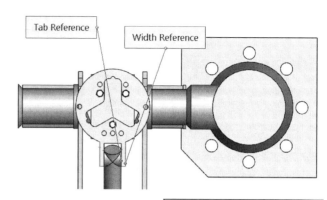

5. **Create** a Flexible state for the Hydraulic and Brace sub-assembly. Note the icon change in the Assembly FeatureManager.

The Hydraulic and Brace assembly is free to translate. Use this ability to translate and to align the end holes of the sub-assembly to the brace of the Welding Arm assembly.

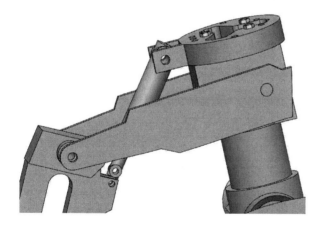

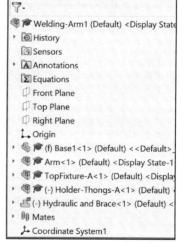

6. **Insert** a Concentric mate between the two cylindrical faces as illustrated.

7. **Insert** a (25 degree) Angle mate between the flat face of the Thong holder and the top face of the Fixture. Note: the angle dimension is referenced from the top of the Fixture.

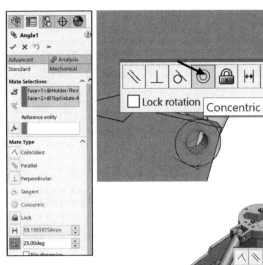

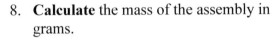

8. **Calculate** the mass of the assembly in grams.

9. **Enter 4613.33** grams. Always enter the needed decimal places in the answer field.

10. **Calculate** the center of mass (mm) relative to Coordinate System1.

11. **Enter** the center of mass (mm) in the three blank fields. You need to be within .5% of the answer to get this question correct.

    X = -92.11

    Y = 40.93

    Z = 134.60

12. **Save** the assembly.

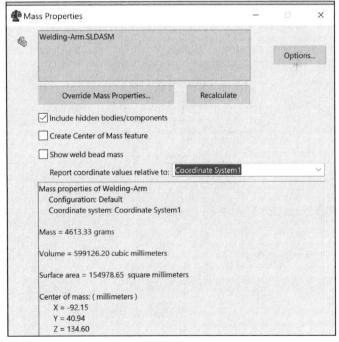

💡 Use the Measure tool to confirm your Angle mate dimension.

💡 During the exam, you will be forced into an error situation.

A question in this segment could be - download and open the attached components (Spring Pin Slotted _AI_1-5, Dowel Pin_AI, and Spring Pin Slotted_AI_5).

Insert the Spring Pin Slotted _AI_1-5 component, the Dowel Pin_AI component, and the Spring Pin Slotted_AI_5 component into the Welding Arm assembly.

Set the proper faces (mates) as indicated in the images.

Insert Concentric and Width mates.

Modify the dimension of the Spring Pin Slotted _AI_1-5 component to be flush with the outside face of the Support Arms (50mm). Calculate the mass of the Welding Arm assembly in grams. Calculate the Center of mass using the new Coordinate System.

Provided Information:

Unit system: MMGS (millimeter, gram, second)

Decimal places: 2

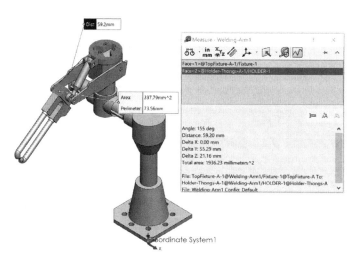

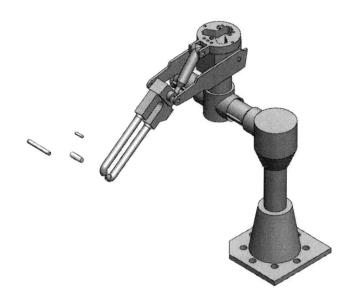

Spring Pin Slotted _AI_1-5

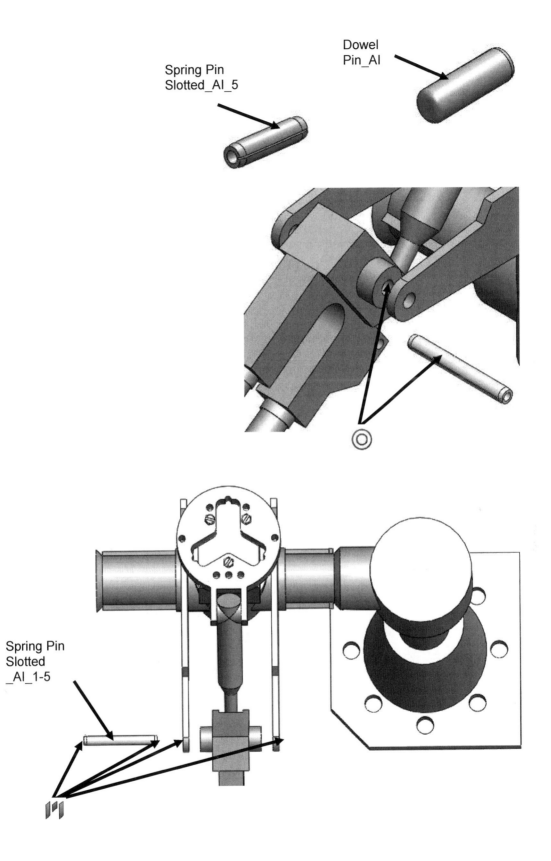

Spring Pin
Slotted_Al_5

Dowel
Pin_Al

Spring Pin
Slotted
_Al_1-5

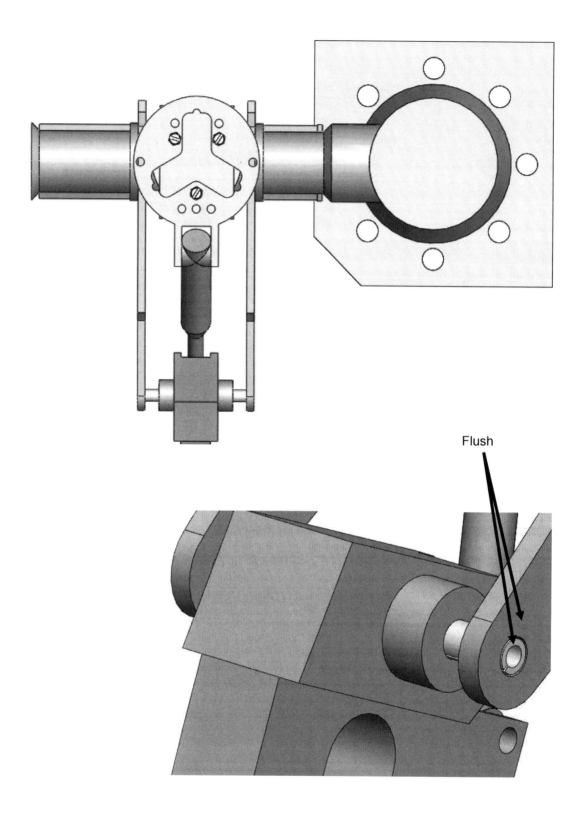

Flush

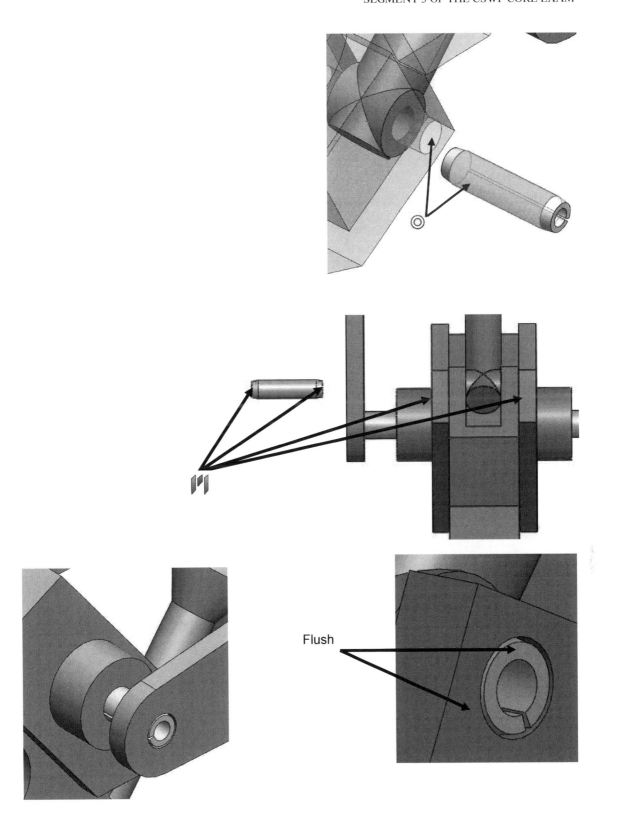

Flush

Page 3 - 35

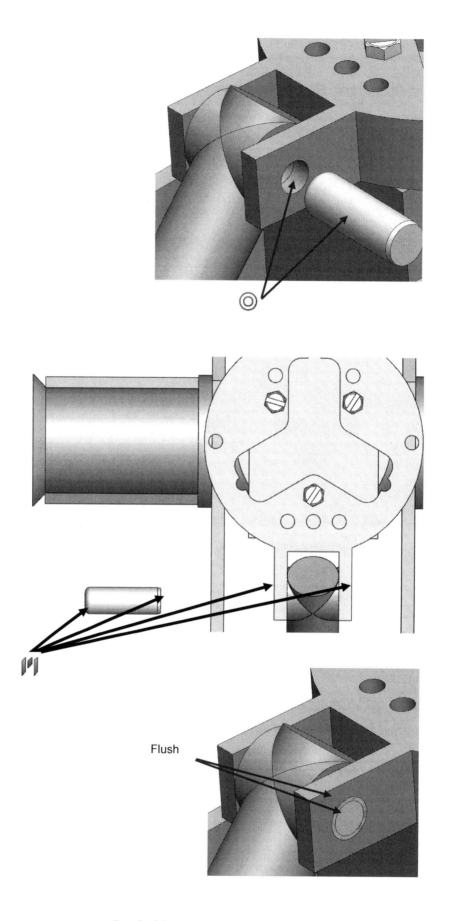

Flush

Let's begin.

1. **Insert** the Spring Pin Slotted
   _AI_1-5 component, the Dowel
   Pin_AI component, and the Spring
   Pin Slotted_AI_5 component (from
   Segment 3 Initial/Initial 5 - add pins
   folder) into the Welder Arm
   assembly.

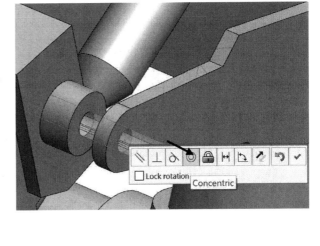

2. **Create** a Concentric mate between
   the outside cylindrical face of the
   Spring Pin Slotted _AI_1-5
   component and inside cylindrical
   face of the TopFixture-A
   component.

3. **Create** a Width mate between the
   Spring Pin Slotted _AI_1-5
   component and the two support
   arms of the assembly. Note: the
   Spring Pin is not flush with the two support arms.

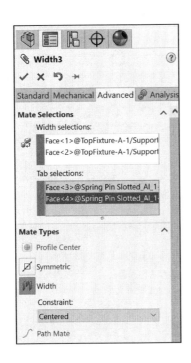

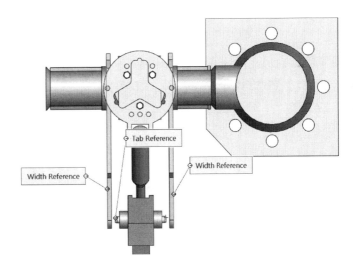

4. **Modify** the Spring Pin Slotted _AI_1-5 component length dimension to 50mm (flush) with the outside face of the two support arms of the assembly. It is important that you know how to modify dimensions of a component inside an assembly for the exam.

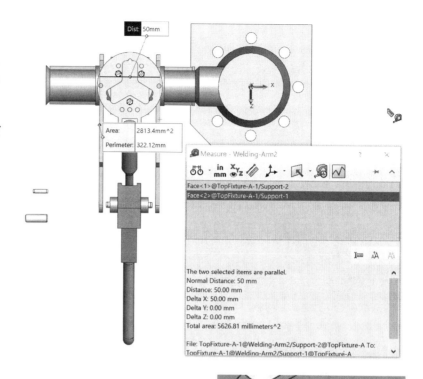

5. If needed, uncheck the **Make this folder the default search location for Toolbox components** under System Options.

6. **Create** a Concentric mate between the outside cylindrical face of the Spring Pin Slotted_AI_5 component and the inside cylindrical face of the Holder-Thongs-A component. Note - use the Select Other option if needed.

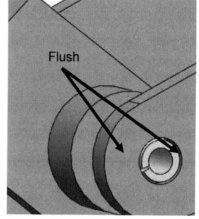

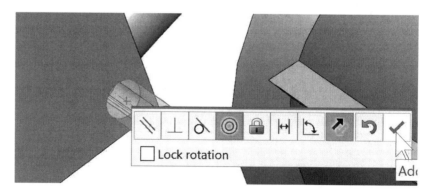

7. **Create** a Width mate between the Spring Pin Slotted_AI_5 component and the two faces of the Holder-Thong of the assembly. The faces are flush.

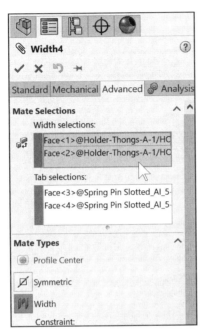

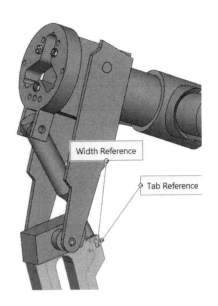

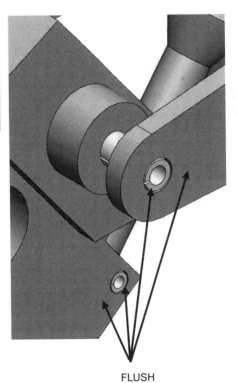

FLUSH

8. **Create** a Concentric mate between the outside cylindrical face of the Dowel Pin_AI component and the inside cylindrical face of the TopFixture-A component.

9. **Create** a Width mate between the Dowel Pin_AI component and the two faces. The faces are flush.

10. **Calculate** the mass of the assembly in grams.

11. **Enter 4623.00** grams. Always enter the needed decimal places in the answer field.

Another question could be - calculate the center of mass (mm) of the Welding Arm assembly relative to Coordinate System1.

12. **Calculate** the center of mass (mm) relative to the Coordinate System1. Enter the center of mass in the three blank fields in the exam.

   X = -92.28

   Y = 40.82

   Z = 134.84

13. **Save** the assembly.

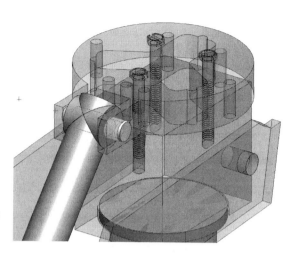

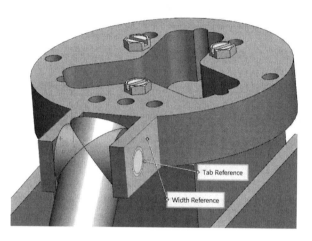

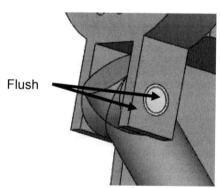

Flush

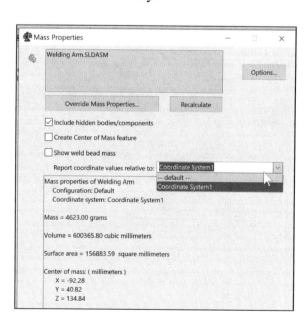

A question in this segment could be - download and open the attached component (BaseB).

Replace the Base1 component with the BaseB component. Note: BaseB is located in the Segment 3 Initial/Initial 5 - replace base folder

Mate the Arm to BaseB using the same mates as with the Base1 component.

Maintain the same mates of the rest of the components as previously directed.

Redefine Coordinate System1 with BaseB as illustrated.

Using the created coordinate system as the Output Coordinate System, calculate the center of mass (mm) of the assembly.

Another question could be - calculate the mass of the assembly in grams.

Provided Information:

Unit system: MMGS (millimeter, gram, second)

Decimal places: 2

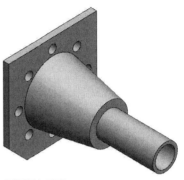

Base1 part

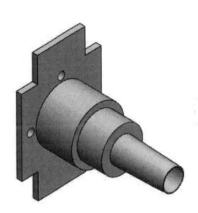

BaseB part

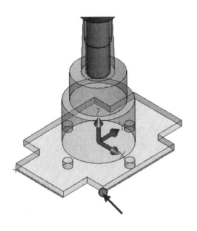

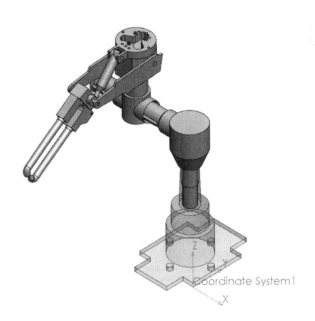

Let's begin.

Replace the Base1 component in the Welding Arm assembly.

1. **Right-click** Base1 in the Assembly FeatureManager.

2. Click **Replace Components**.

3. **Browse** to the location that you downloaded the book models (Segment 3 Initial/Initial 5 - replace base folder).

4. **Double-click** BaseB.

5. Click **OK** from the PropertyManager.

The What's Wrong dialog box is displayed. Isolate the Base component. This section presents a representation of the types of questions that you will see in this segment of the exam Depending on your selection of faces and order of components inserted into the top-level assembly, your error messages may vary. Address errors as needed.

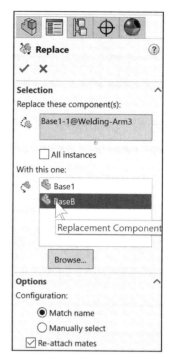

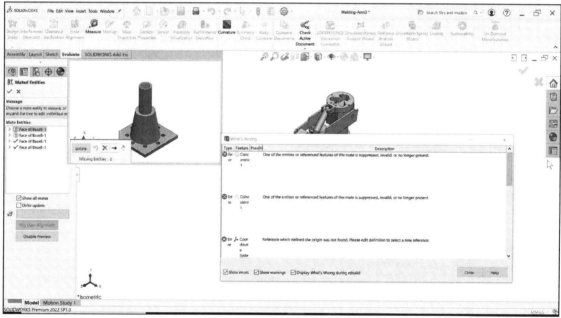

Replace the missing faces to address the mate errors.

6. **Click** Isolate.

7. Click **Selected Entity**. The Base1 part is displayed in the isolate window. The BaseB part is displayed in the Graphics window.

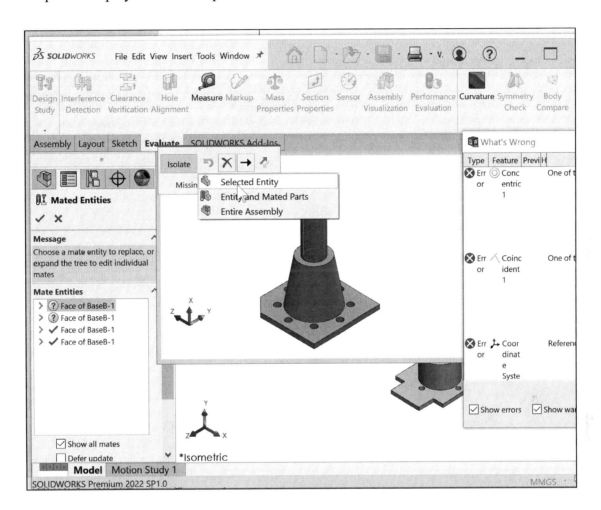

8. **Click** the inside cylindrical face of BaseB as illustrated. The Concentric1 error is removed.

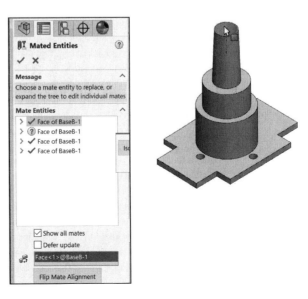

9. **Expand** the Face of BaseB-1 Mate Entities.

10. **Click** Coincident1.

11. **Click** inside the flat bottom circular face of BaseB as illustrated. The error is removed.

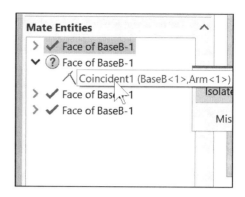

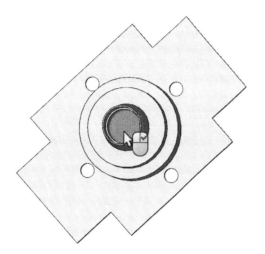

12. **Click** Entire Assembly from the Isolate box. The arm is in the correct orientation. If not, click the Flip Mate Alignment button.

13. **Click** OK from the Mated Entities PropertyManager. There is still an error with the coordinate system.

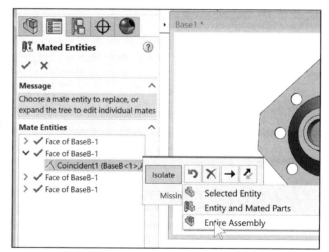

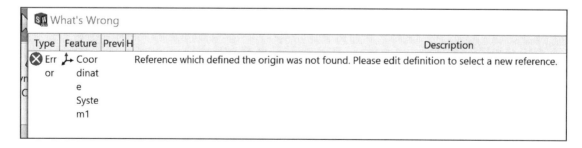

Type	Feature	Previ	H	Description
Err or	Coor dinat e Syste m1			Reference which defined the origin was not found. Please edit definition to select a new reference.

Confirm the position of the Arm component inside the Welding Arm assembly. Use the Change Transparency tool or a section view to confirm the location of mated components in the assembly.

14. **Right-click** Change Transparency from the BaseB component in the Assembly PropertyManager.

15. **Close** all dialog boxes.

Address the error for Coordinate System1. Redefine the vertex.

16. **Edit** Coordinate System1.

17. **Click** the bottom right front vertex on the BaseB component as illustrated.

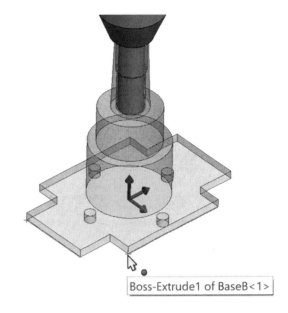

Boss-Extrude1 of BaseB<1>

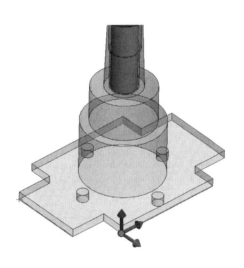

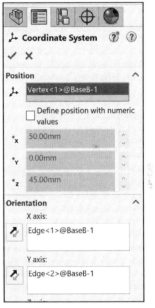

18. **Calculate** the mass of the assembly in grams.

19. **Enter 5251.51** grams. Always enter the needed decimal places in the answer field.

20. **Calculate** the center of mass (mm) relative to the redefined Coordinate System1. Enter the center of mass in the three blank fields in the exam.

X = -87.30

Y = 36.84

Z = 130.27

21. **Save** the assembly.

☀ Depending on your selection of faces and order of components inserted into the top-level assembly, your error messages may vary.

☀ Knowledge of Gear Mates is required to address ratio movement in the exam.

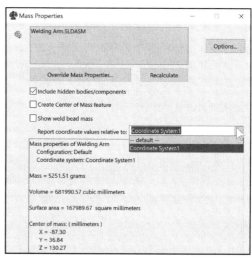

-Create or remove any necessary mates to allow the opening and movement of the Claw1 assembly as shown. Do not modify the position of any of the components as defined in the previous question until instructed below

Note: The two Arm_Gear parts should move in a ratio of 32mm:54mm with respect to each other as shown in the image

Note2: The gears are currently not sized true to scale

Segment 3 of the CSWP CORE exam - Additional Practice Problems

In this section, there are fewer step-by-step procedures than above. Use the provided initial and final models with the rollback bar if needed.

Create an assembly (Bench Vise) starting with the Bench Vise-Base component.

Some components in the exam are modeled by you and others will be supplied to you.

Load the Testing client and read the instructions. Create a folder to save your working models.

The first question in this segment is instructional.

The second question can be - download the Bench Vise-Base component and create the Bench Vise assembly.

Insert and orientate the Bench Vise-Base component as illustrated below with the Red tab in the front location.

Provided information:

Units: IPS (inch, pound, second)

Decimal Places: 2

Part Origin: Arbitrary

All holes through all unless shown otherwise.

There are no inferences.

The Top Plane of the assembly is perpendicular with the Front Plane of the Bench Vise-Base component.

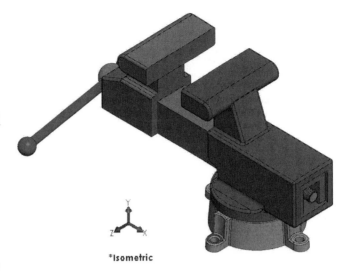

*Isometric

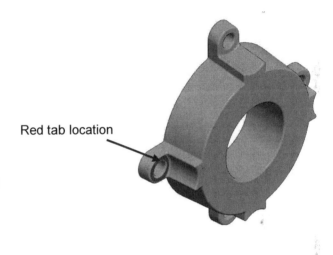

Red tab location

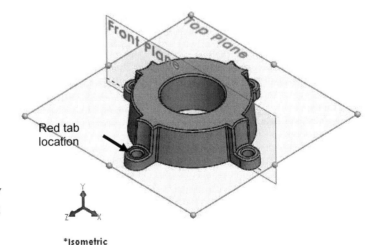

Red tab location

*Isometric

A question in this segment could be - what is the center of mass of the Bench Vise-Base component in the assembly?

During the exam, SOLIDWORKS will provide a part to create that is not orientated correctly in the assembly. Knowledge of component orientation in an assembly is required along with creating coordinate systems.

Let's begin.

1. **Create** an assembly document.

2. **Insert** the Bench Vise-Base component (Segment 3 Initial/Bench Vise Parts folder). Fix the Bench Vise-Base component to the origin of the assembly. Set document units and precision.

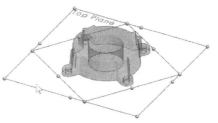

There are numerous ways to modify the orientation of a component in an assembly document that is fixed to the origin.

Use the Float and Mate tools in the next section. Re-orientate the Bench Vise-Base component. Fully define the component in the Assembly document.

3. **Float** the part.

4. **Re-orientate** the assembly as needed. Create a Coincident mate between the Right Plane of the Bench Vise-Base component and the Top Plane of the assembly.

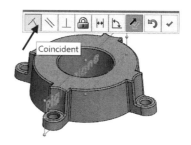

5. **Click** the Aligned option if needed.

Create two additional Coincident mates.

6. **Create** a Coincident mate between the Right Plane of the Assembly and the Top Plane of the Bench Vise-Base component.

Another mate is needed to fully define the component.

7. **Create** a Coincident mate between the Front Plane of the Assembly and the Front Plane of the Bench Vise-Base component. The Bench Vise-Base component is fully defined in the Assembly document.

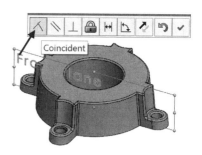

You can also rotate the Bench Vise-Base component in the assembly using the Rotate Component tool (about Y&X).

8. **Calculate** the center of mass in inches of the Bench Vise-Base component in the assembly. Note: All answers in the CSWP exam use the MMGS unit system.

9. **Enter** the center of mass in the three blank fields (inches). You need to be within .5% of the answer to get this question correct.

X = 0.00

Y = 0.59

Z = 0.00

10. **Save** the assembly in an Isometric view.

11. **Name** the assembly Bench Vise.

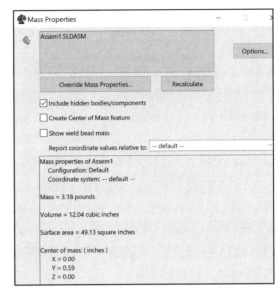

SOLIDWORKS Mass Properties calculates the center of mass for every model. At every instant of time, there is a unique location (x, y, z) in space that is the average position of the systems mass.

There are numerous ways to build the model in this section. A goal is to display different design intents and techniques.

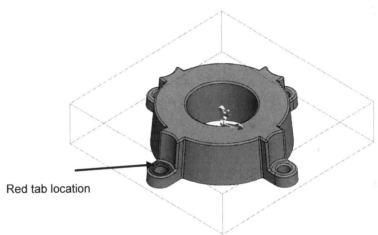

Red tab location

Question 2:

A question in this segment could be - download and open the Bench Vise-Main Body sub assembly. Insert the Bench Vise-Main Body sub assembly into the Bench Vise assembly.

Position the Bench Vise-Main Body assembly with respect to the Bench Vise-Base component.

All parts are Coincident and there are no inferences.

Insert all needed mates.

What is the center of mass of the Bench Vise assembly?

Provided Information:

Unit system: IPS (inch, pound, second)

Decimal places: 2

SOLIDWORKS provides symbols to indicate a Parallel mate, Width mate, Coincident mate, etc. in the exam.

Take your time to review the drawing views and to understand the required mates between each component.

In this example a Parallel mate is needed between the Front Plane of the Bench Vise-Main Body sub assembly and the Front Plane of the Bench Vise assembly.

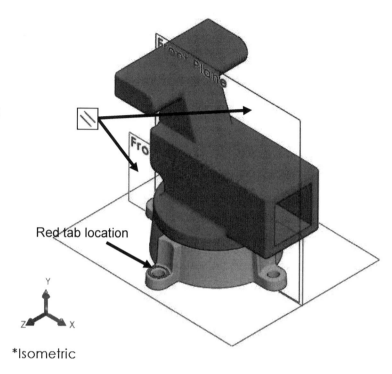

Red tab location

*Isometric

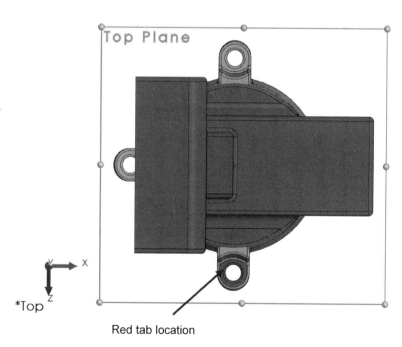

Red tab location

Let's begin.

Insert the Bench Vise-Main Body sub assembly.

14. **Insert** the Bench Vise-Main Body sub assembly (from the Segment 3 Initial/Bench Vise Parts folder) into the Bench Vise assembly.

15. **Insert** a Coincident mate between the temporary axis of the Bench Vise-Base component and the temporary axis of the Bench Vise-Main Jaw Body sub assembly.

It is good practice to save frequently and to rename the part or assembly if you need to go back during the exam.

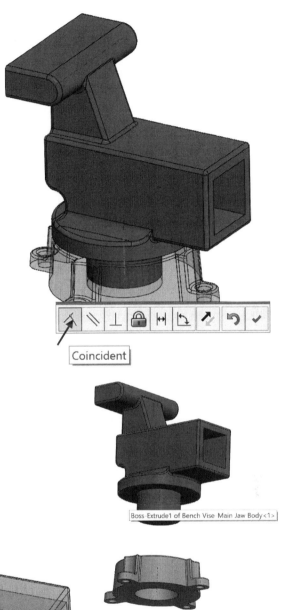

16. **Insert** a Coincident mate between the top face of the Bench Vise-Base component and the bottom face of the Bench Vise-Main body. The Bench Vise is free to rotate.

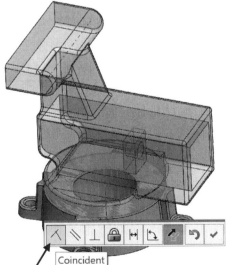

Next, restrict the rotation of the vise.

17. **Insert** a Parallel mate between the Front Plane of the Bench Vise-Main Body sub assembly and the Front Plane of the Bench Vise assembly.

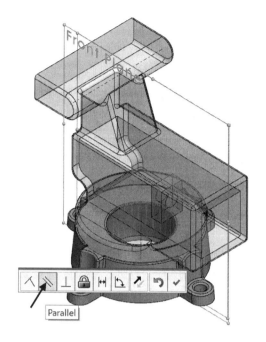

18. **Calculate** the center of mass of the Bench Vise assembly.

19. **Enter** the center of mass (inch) in the three blank fields.

   X = 0.00

   Y = 2.33

   Z = 0.00

20. **Save** the assembly.

There are numerous ways to address the question in this section. A goal is to display different design intents and techniques.

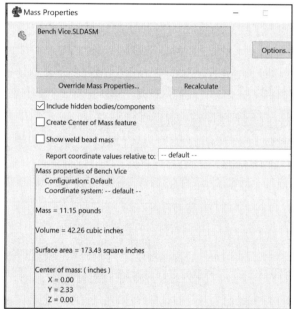

Question 3:

A question in this segment could be – Insert the Bench Vise-Sliding Jaw and Bench Vise-Threaded rod components.

All parts are Coincident and there are no inferences.

There is a 2in distance between the face of the Bench Vise-Sliding Jaw and the face of the Bench Vise-Main Jaw body.

The Bench Vise-Threaded rod is free to rotate about its axis.

Calculate the Normal Distance of X. X is the distance from the end of the threaded rod to the back of the threaded rod holder.

Calculate the mass of the final assembly.

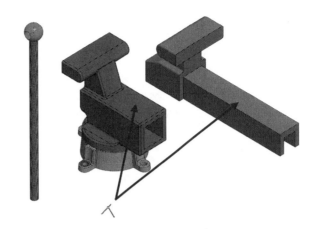

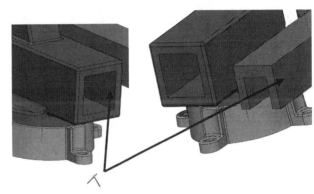

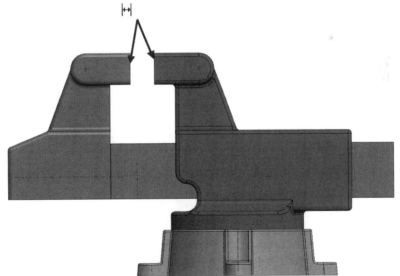

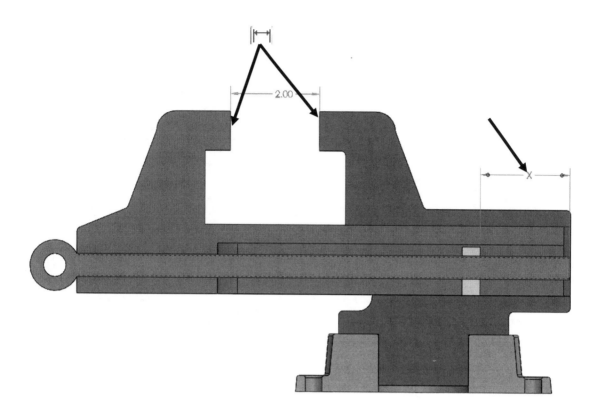

Provided Information:

Unit system: IPS (inch, pound, second)

Decimal places: 2

Let's begin.

21. **Insert** the Bench Vise-Sliding Jaw and the Bench Vise-Threaded rod (from the Segment 3 Initial/Bench Vise Parts folder) into the Bench Vise assembly.

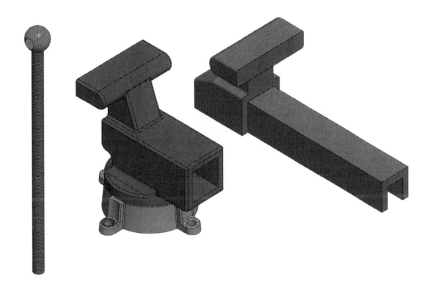

22. **Insert** two Coincident mates to mate the Bench Vise-Sliding Jaw into the Bench Vise-Main jaw body.

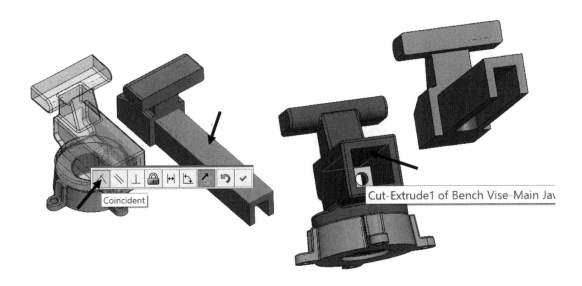

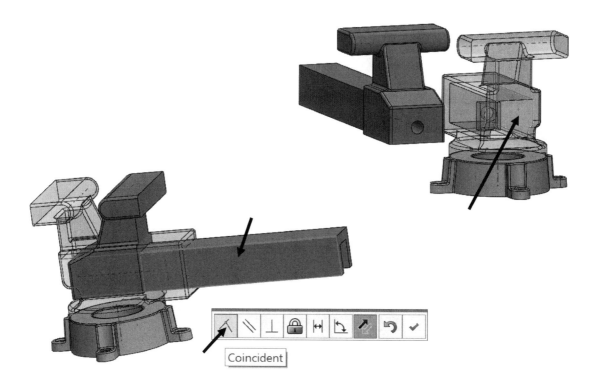

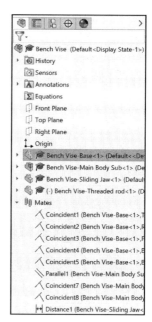

23. **Insert** a Distance mate 2in between the face of the Bench Vise-Sliding Jaw and the face of the Bench Vise-Main Jaw body jaws of the vise.

24. **Save** the assembly.

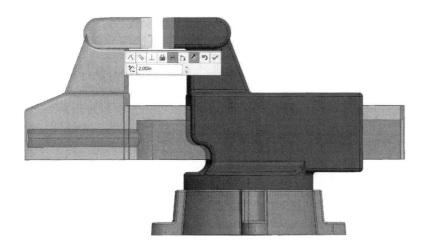

25. **Insert** a Coincident mate between the edge of the Bench Vise-Threaded rod and the hole edge of the Bench Vise-Sliding Jaw component. The Threaded rod is free to rotate about its axis.

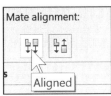

Calculate the Normal Distance of X shown in the image. X is the distance from the end of the threaded rod to the back of the threaded rod holder.

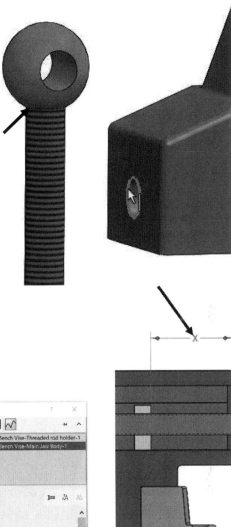

26. **Apply** the Measure tool. Measure the distance between the end of the threaded rod to the back of the threaded rod holder.

27. **Enter 2.00** for the answer to this question. Always enter the needed decimal places in the answer field.

28. **Save** the assembly.

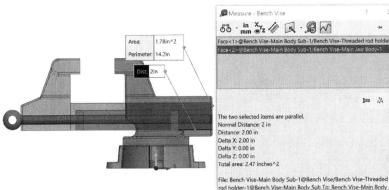

Question 4:

A question in this segment could be - Insert the Bench Vise Handle into the assembly. Mate the rod. X is an 80-degree Angle mate between the Right Plane of the Bench Vise-Handle and the Top Plane of the assembly. Y is 0 distance (Collision Detection tool) between the Bench Vise-Handel and the Bench Vise-Threaded rod. Calculate the center of mass of the assembly.

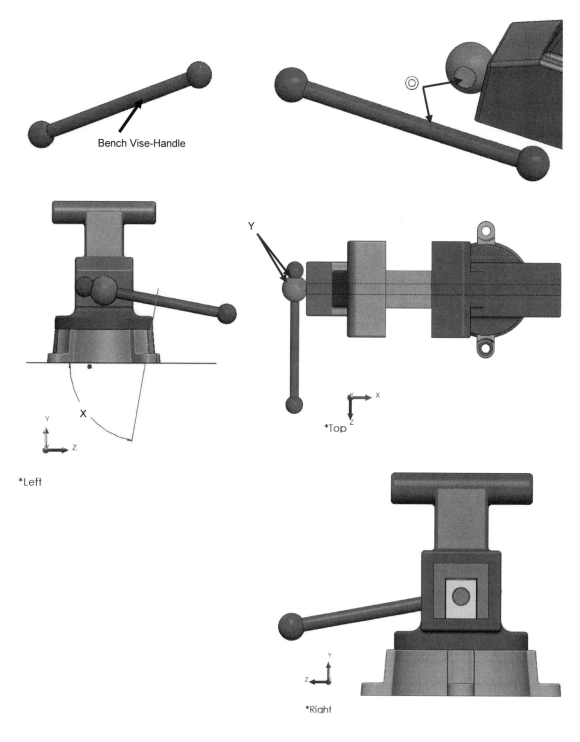

To define the axial translation, apply the
Move tool with Collision Detection to
determine the position. The location is where
the ball of the handle is Coincident with the
hole in the threaded rod.

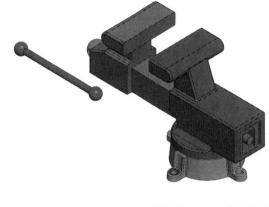

💡 Knowledge of Collision Detection and
the Measure tool is required for this section.

Provided Information:

Unit system: IPS (inch, pound, second)

Decimal places: 2

Let's begin.

29. **Insert** the Bench Vise-Handle
from the (Segment 3 Initial/Bench
Vise Parts folder) into the Bench
Vise assembly.

30. **Insert** a Concentric mate between
the face of the hole of the
threaded rod and the cylindrical
face of the handle.

31. **Insert** an 80-degree Angle mate
between the Right Plane of the
Bench Vise-Handle and the Top
Plane of the assembly. Apply the
Flip Dimension option if needed.

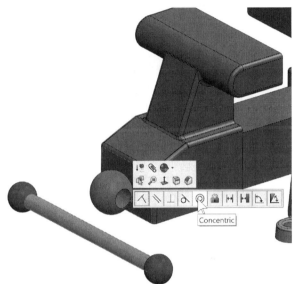

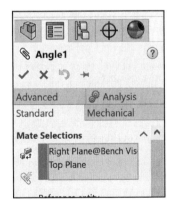

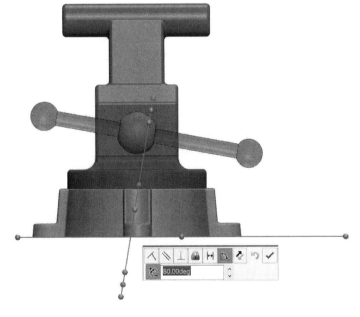

32. **Activate** Collision detection from the Rotate Component PropertyManager.

33. **Calculate** the center of mass of the assembly.

34. **Enter** the center of mass in the three blank fields. Always enter the needed decimal places in the answer field.

X = -1.86

Y = 2.85

Z = 0.03

35. **Save** the assembly.

There are numerous ways to build the assembly in this section. A goal is to display different design intents and techniques.

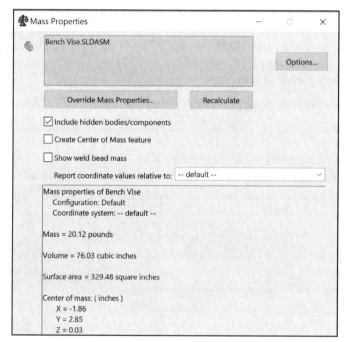

Question 5:

A question in this segment could be - replace the Bench Vise-Base component with the Bench Vise-Base2 component.

Mate the Bench Vise to the Bench Vise-Base2 component using the same mates as with the Bench Vise-Base.

Maintain the same mates of the rest of the components as previously directed. Address all mate errors.

There are no interferences in the assembly.

Calculate the center of mass of the assembly.

Provided Information:

Unit system: MMGS (millimeter, gram, second)

Decimal places: 2

Let's begin.

36. Replace the Bench Vise-Base component in the Bench Vise assembly. **Right-click** Bench Vise-Base in the Assembly FeatureManager. Click Replace Components.

37. **Browse** to the location that you downloaded the models (Segment 3 Initial/Bench Vise Parts folder).

38. **Double-click** Bench Vise-Base 2.

39. Click **OK** from the Replace PropertyManager.

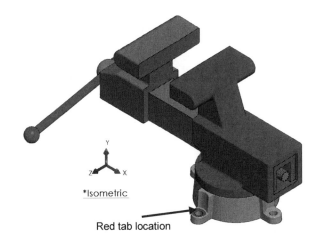

Red tab location

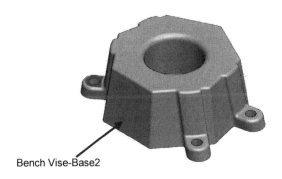

Bench Vise-Base2

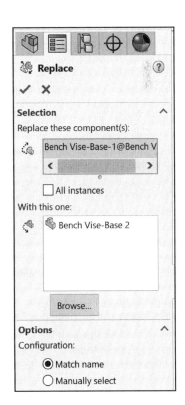

🔅 Unselect the Re-attach mates box in the Replace PropertyManager to manually address all needed mates.

The What's Wrong dialog box is displayed. Isolate the Base component. This section presents a representation of the types of questions that you will see in this segment of the exam

Depending on your selection of faces and order of components inserted into the top-level assembly, your error messages may vary.

Address errors as needed. Address mate issues as needed. The following is not a step-by-step procedure to the final solution. There are many ways to replace a component in an assembly and to address the mate errors.

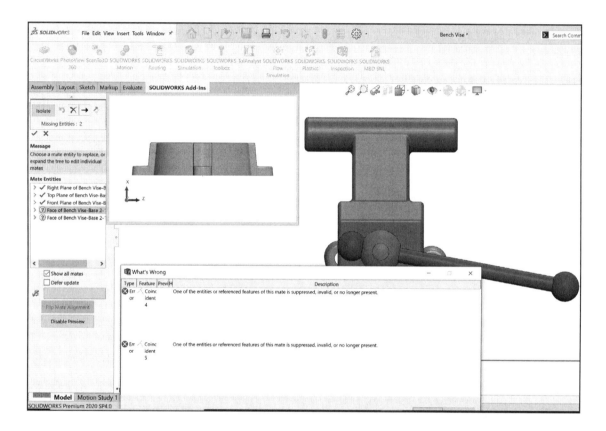

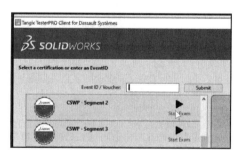

If your school is an academic certification provider, your instructor can allocate a free exam credit for the CSWP (Segment 1, Segment 2 or Segment 3). The instructor will require your .edu email address.

Replace the missing faces to address the mate errors.

40. **Click** Isolate. Select **Entity and Mated Parts**.

41. **Delete** the mate between the Top Plane of the Bench Vise-Base 2 component (Concident2) and the Right Plane of the assembly.

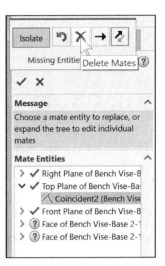

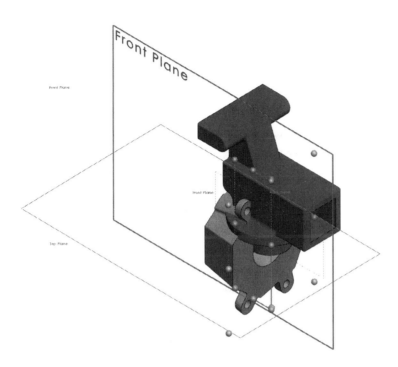

42. **Modify** the Coincident mate that is currently with the Right Plane of the Bench Vise-Base2 and the Top Plane of the assembly to the Top Plane of the Bench Vise-Base2 component with the Top Plane of the assembly.

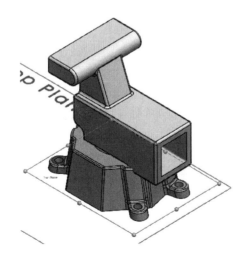

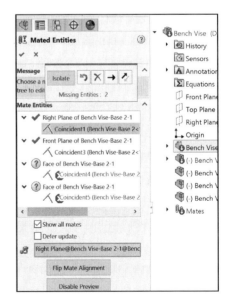

43. **Expand** the second Mate Entity error as illustrated.

44. **Click** Coincident5. It has a missing reference with the top face of Bench Vise-Base. **Select** the Top face of Bench Vise-Base 2.

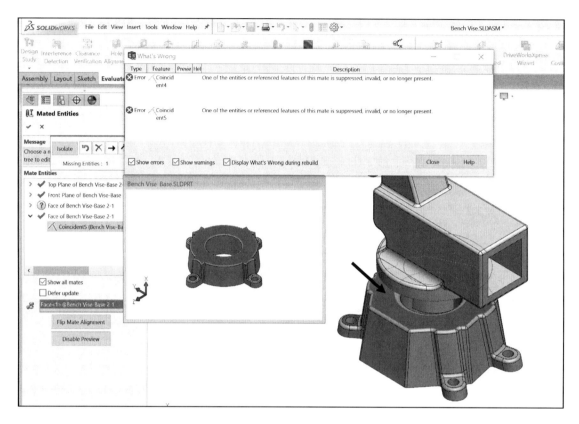

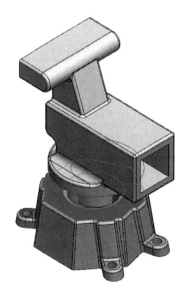

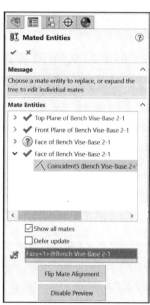

45. **Expand** the first Mate Entity error.

46. **Click** Coincident4. Replace the missing reference.

47. **Select** the temporary axis of Bench Vise-Base 2.

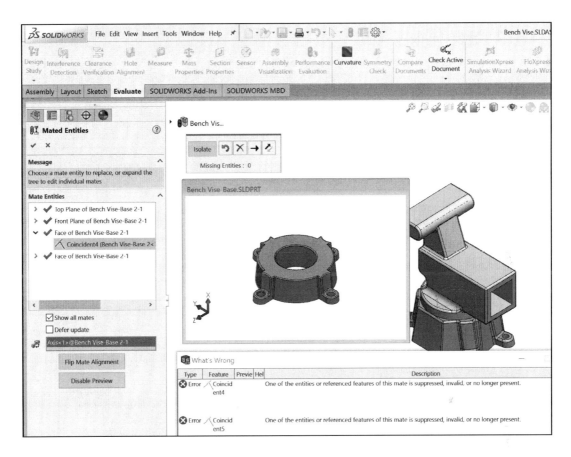

48. **Click** OK from the Mated Entities PropertyManager.

49. **Insert** a Coincident mate between the Right Plane of the Bench Vise-Base2 and the Right Plane of the assembly.

50. **Address** any additional mates to fully constrain the assembly.

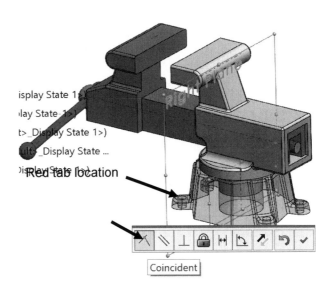

51. **Modify** the assembly documents to MMGS.

52. **Calculate** the center of mass in mm of the assembly relative to the location of the red tab location on the Bench Vise Base2 component.

53. **Enter** the center of mass (mm) in the three blank fields.

  X = -40.13

  Y = 79.94

  Z = 0.67

54. **Save** the assembly. Note: Check the interference between the Bench Vise-Handle (Coincident) and the hole in the Bench Vise-Threaded rod if you are off in the Z direction.

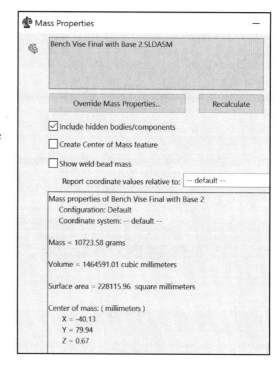

There are numerous ways to address the question in this section. A goal is to display different design intents and techniques.

You are finished with this section. Good luck on segment 3 of the CSWP exam.

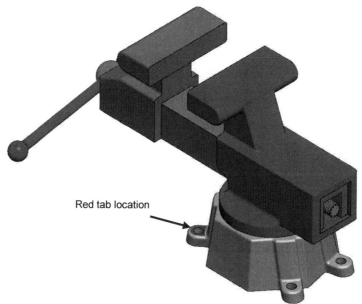

Red tab location

At the end of the exam, view the Summary dialog box.

Press the End Examination button only if you are finished. A total score of 77 out of 109 or better is required to pass Segment 3.

Pro. - CSWP Segment 3 of 3   ×

Summary

Question (double-click to go to)		Points	State
1	- This text describes the problem that must be solved in this proble...	5	Answered
2	- Create the RA assembly	8	Answered
3	- Insert Actuator1 into RA Main Assembly	8	Answered
4	- Insert assembly X1 into RA main assembly	8	Answered
5	- Insert assembly X2 into RA main assembly	8	Answered
6	- Rotate assembly X2 and Collision Detection	8	Answered
7	- Create Claw1 assembly	8	Answered
8	- Claw1 opening	8	Answered
9	- Insert Claw1 into X3 assembly	8	Answered
10	- Insert assembly X3 into RA main assembly	8	Answered
11	- Modify X3 Mass Properties	8	Answered
12	- Mate Claw with sketch S1	8	Answered
13	- Interference detection	8	Answered
14	- Replace Base part	8	Answered

Always save your models to verify your results.

Note: If you fail this segment of the exam, you need to wait 14 days before you can retake that same segment. In that time, you can take another segment.

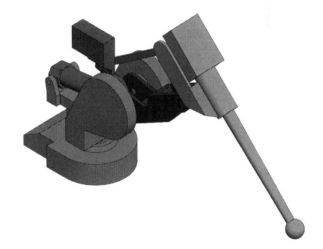

Notes:

Notes:

Appendix

SOLIDWORKS Keyboard Shortcuts

Below are some of the pre-defined keyboard shortcuts in SOLIDWORKS:

Action:	Key Combination:
Model Views	
Rotate the model horizontally or vertically	**Arrow** keys
Rotate the model horizontally or vertically 90 degrees	**Shift + Arrow** keys
Rotate the model clockwise or counterclockwise	**Alt** + left of right **Arrow** keys
Pan the model	**Ctrl + Arrow** keys
Magnifying glass	**g**
Zoom in	**Shift + z**
Zoom out	**z**
Zoom to fit	**f**
Previous view	**Ctrl + Shift + z**
View Orientation	
View Orientation menu	**Spacebar**
Front view	**Ctrl + 1**
Back view	**Ctrl + 2**
Left view	**Ctrl + 3**
Right view	**Ctrl + 4**
Top view	**Ctrl + 5**
Bottom view	**Ctrl + 6**
Isometric view	**Ctrl + 7**
NormalTo view	**Ctrl + 8**
Selection Filters	
Filter edges	**e**
Filter vertices	**v**
Filter faces	**x**
Toggle Selection Filter toolbar	**F5**
Toggle selection filters on/off	**F6**
File menu items	
New SOLIDWORKS document	**Ctrl + n**
Open document	**Ctrl + o**
Open From Web Folder	**Ctrl + w**
Make Drawing from Part	**Ctrl + d**
Make Assembly from Part	**Ctrl + a**
Save	**Ctrl +s**
Print	**Ctrl + p**
Additional items	
Access online help inside of PropertyManager or dialog box	**F1**
Rename an item in the FeatureManager design tree	**F2**

Action:	Key Combination:
Rebuild the model	**Ctrl + b**
Force rebuild - Rebuild the model and all its features	**Ctrl + q**
Redraw the screen	**Ctrl + r**
Cycle between open SOLIDWORKS document	**Ctrl + Tab**
Line to arc/arc to line in the Sketch	**a**
Undo	**Ctrl + z**
Redo	**Ctrl + y**
Cut	**Ctrl + x**
Copy	**Ctrl + c**
Paste	**Ctrl + v**
Delete	**Delete**
Next window	**Ctrl + F6**
Close window	**Ctrl + F4**
View previous tools	**s**
Selects all text inside an Annotations text box	**Ctrl + a**

In a sketch, the **Esc** key un-selects geometry items currently selected in the Properties box and Add Relations box.

In the model, the **Esc** key closes the PropertyManager and cancels the selections.

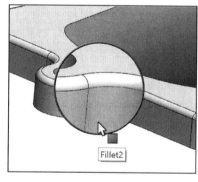

Use the **g** key to activate the Magnifying glass tool. Use the Magnifying glass tool to inspect a model and make selections without changing the overall view.

Use the **s** key to view/access previous command tools in the Graphics window.

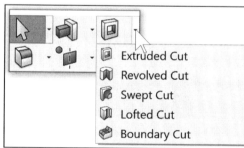

Modeling - Best Practices

Best practices are simply ways of bringing about better results in easier, more reliable ways. The Modeling - Best Practice list is a set of rules helpful for new users and users who are trying to experiment with the limits of the software.

These rules are not inflexible, but conservative starting places; they are concepts that you can default to, but that can be broken if you have good reason. The following is a list of suggested best practices:

- Create a folder structure (parts, drawings, assemblies, simulations, etc.). Organize into project or file folders.

- Construct sound document templates. The document template provides the foundation that all models are built on. This is especially important if working with other SOLIDWORKS users on the same project; it will ensure consistency across the project.

- Generate unique part filenames. SOLIDWORKS assemblies and drawings may pick up incorrect references if you use parts with identical names.

- Apply Custom Properties. Custom Properties is a great way to enter text-based information into the SOLIDWORKS parts. Users can view this information from outside the file by using applications such as Windows Explorer, SOLIDWORKS Explorer, and Product Data Management (PDM) applications.

- Understand part orientation. When you create a new part or assembly, the three default Planes (Front, Right and Top) are aligned with specific views. The plane you select for the Base sketch determines the orientation.

- Learn to sketch using automatic relations.

- Limit your usage of the Fixed constraint.

- Add geometric relations, then dimensions in a 2D sketch. This keeps the part from having too many unnecessary dimensions. This also helps to show the design intent of the model. Dimension what geometry you intend to modify or adjust.

- Fully define all sketches in the model. However, there are times when this is not practical, generally when using the Spline tool to create a freeform shape.

- When possible, make relations to sketches or stable reference geometry, such as the Origin or standard planes, instead of edges or faces. Sketches are far more stable than faces, edges, or model vertices, which change their internal ID at the slightest change and may disappear entirely with fillets, chamfers, split lines, and so on.

- Do not dimension to edges created by fillets or other cosmetic or temporary features.

- Apply names to sketches, features, dimensions, and mates that help to make their function clear.

- When possible, use feature fillets and feature patterns rather than sketch fillets and sketch patterns.

- Apply the Shell feature before the Fillet feature, and the inside corners remain perpendicular.

- Apply cosmetic fillets and chamfers last in the modeling procedure.

- Combine fillets into as few fillet features as possible. This enables you to control fillets that need to be controlled separately, such as fillets to be removed and simplified configurations.

- Create a simplified configuration when building very complex parts or working with large assemblies.

- Use symmetry during the modeling process. Utilize feature patterns and mirroring when possible. Think End Conditions.

- Use global variables and equations to control commonly applied dimensions (design intent).

- Add comments to equations to document your design intent. Place a single quote (') at the end of the equation, then enter the comment. Anything after the single quote is ignored when the equation is evaluated.

- Avoid redundant mates. Although SOLIDWORKS allows some redundant mates (all except distance and angle), these mates take longer to solve and make the mating scheme harder to understand and diagnose if problems occur.

- Fix modeling errors in the part or assembly when they occur. Errors cause rebuild time to increase, and if you wait until additional errors exist, troubleshooting will be more difficult.

- Create a Library of Standardized notes and parts.

- Utilize the Rollback bar. Troubleshoot feature and sketch errors from the top of the design tree.

- Determine the static and dynamic behavior of mates in each sub-assembly before creating the top-level assembly.

- Plan the assembly and sub-assemblies in an assembly layout diagram. Group components together to form smaller sub-assemblies.

- When you create an assembly document, the base component should be fixed, fully defined or mated to an axis about the assembly origin.

- In an assembly, group fasteners into a folder at the bottom of the FeatureManager. Suppress fasteners and their assembly patterns to save rebuild time and file size.

- When comparing mass, volume and other properties with assembly visualization, utilize similar units.

- Use limit mates sparingly because they take longer to solve and whenever possible, mate all components to one or two fixed components or references. Long chains of components take longer to solve and are more prone to mate errors.

Helpful On-line Information

The SOLIDWORKS URL:
http://www.SOLIDWORKS.com
contains information on Local
Resellers, Solution Partners,
Certifications, SOLIDWORKS
user's groups and more.

Use the SOLIDWORKS
Resources tab in the Task Pane to
obtain access to Customer Portals,
User Groups, Manufacturers,
Solution Partners, Labs,
3DEXPERIENCE Marketplace, and more.

Helpful on-line SOLIDWORKS information is available from
the following URLs:

- http://www.swugn.org/

List of all SOLIDWORKS User groups.

- https://www.solidworks.com/sw/edu
  cation/certification-programs-cad-
  students.htm

The SOLIDWORKS Academic
Certification Programs.

- http://www.solidworks.com/sw/in
  dustries/education/engineering-
  education-software.htm

The SOLIDWORKS Education
Program:

- To obtain additional
  SOLIDWORKS Certification
  exam information, visit
  https://3dexperience.virtualtester.c
  om/#home

On-line tutorials are for educational
purposes only. Tutorials are
copyrighted by their respective
owners.

SOLIDWORKS Document Types

SOLIDWORKS has three main document file types: Part, Assembly and Drawing, but there are many additional supporting types that you may want to know. Below is a brief list of these supporting file types:

Design Documents	Description
.sldprt	SOLIDWORKS Part document
.slddrw	SOLIDWORKS Drawing document
.sldasm	SOLIDWORKS Assembly document

Templates and Formats	Description
.asmdot	Assembly Template
.asmprp	Assembly Template Custom Properties tab
.drwdot	Drawing Template
.drwprp	Drawing Template Custom Properties tab
.prtdot	Part Template
.prtprp	Part Template Custom Properties tab
.sldtbt	General Table Template
.slddrt	Drawing Sheet Template
.sldbombt	Bill of Materials Template (Table-based)
.sldholtbt	Hole Table Template
.sldrevbt	Revision Table Template
.sldwldbt	Weldment Cutlist Template
.xls	Bill of Materials Template (Excel-based)

Library Files	Description
.sldlfp	Library Part file
.sldblk	Blocks

Other	Description
.sldstd	Drafting standard
.sldmat	Material Database
.sldclr	Color Palette File
.xls	Sheet metal gauge table